Mistakes

page 21
    35
    48

The Princess in the Mirror

THE PRINCESS
IN THE MIRROR

Suzanne Lowry

Chatto & Windus · London

By the same author

THE GUILT CAGE
THE YOUNG FOGEY HANDBOOK

Published in 1985 by
Chatto & Windus Ltd
40 William IV Street
London WC2N 4DF

British Library Cataloguing in Publication Data

Lowry, Suzanne
    The princess in the mirror.
    1. Diana, *Princess of Wales*   2. Great Britain –
    Princess and princesses – Biography
    I. Title
    941.085'092'4   DA591.A45D5

ISBN 0-7011-2951-4

Photoset by Rowland Phototypesetting Ltd
Bury St Edmunds, Suffolk
Printed in Great Britain by
Redwood Burn Ltd,
Trowbridge, Wiltshire

Contents

not worth
reading !
except to
pick out the
bits on
Diana

Acknowledgements

The author and publishers are grateful to the following for permission to reproduce photographs and illustrations:

London Express News and Feature Services: frontispiece; Camera Press: p. 13; David Bailey (Sunday Times Fashion Archive, Bath Museums Service/Times Newspapers Ltd): p. 22; Peter Abbey (Camera Press Ltd): pp. 27, 28; Dorothy Wilding (Camera Press Ltd): p. 29; Anthony Crickmay (Camera Press Ltd): p. 37; Norman Parkinson (Camera Press Ltd): p. 41; John Shelley (J. S. Library International): p. 42; Anwar Hussein: pp. 49, 75, 105, 143; Times Newspapers Ltd: pp. 56; Syndication International: p. 65; Tim Graham (Tim Graham Picture Library): pp. 71, 139; Nicolla Hewitt: p. 83; Martin Brading: p. 85; Lionel Cherrault (Camera Press Ltd): pp. 91 (*left*), 101; *Slimming* Magazine: p. 91 (*right*); Lord Snowdon (Camera Press Ltd): pp. 96, 129, 135; Alan Davidson (Alpha): p. 100; Frank Powolny (Kobal Collection): p. 108; David Newell-Smith (*Observer*): p. 109; Joanne O'Brien (Format Photographers): p. 115; Posy Simmonds (A. D. Peters Ltd): pp. 126–7; Brian Aris (Duncan Paul Associates): p. 137.

List of Illustrations

Prelude

By the end of the 1970s the loyal British art of royal-watching was in the doldrums. The Queen's Silver Jubilee celebrations in 1977 – street parties, souvenirs, flags, walkabouts – had reconfirmed the deep popular esteem in which the Queen of England was, and is, held. But no one could have claimed that the House of Windsor was at its most charismatic.

The central players in the drama were middle-ageing, some more gracefully than others; of the younger generation, only Prince Charles and Princess Anne were fully on stage, and neither seemed to know their lines. Charles appeared hesitant and self-doubting and unable to find a wife. Anne seemed to care more about horses than people, and was a little too unengagingly frank and gutsy for press and public taste. The bit players verged on the Ruritanian, or were dull to the point of invisibility. Even the high point of the Jubilee, in which the great golden coach was dusted off and trundled out for the first time since Coronation Day, had a touch of cosy bathos about it when the Queen emerged from its baroque shell in a neat pink coat and hat and the famous handbag swinging from one arm. It was a perfect encapsulation of the current royal image: suburban virtues wrapped up in pomp and circumstance.

The monarchy was not under threat, but, as dynasts, critics and, above all, editors and photographers might have agreed, its mythology needed a shot of adrenalin that only New Blood and a thumping good, unscandalous love story could provide. From a constitutional, personal and marketing point of view then – as well as deep in the emotional gut of the nation – it was agreed that Prince Charles must marry: the heir must have an heir.

The Prince himself seemed to agree, but he was not, of course, allowed to pursue the objective – nor the object – in private. The dogged hacks maintained their vigils and exhortations, vetting every blonde as a prospective bride the minute she appeared at a polo match or race meeting, or was even seen 'chatting' to him. But as girl after girl, and rumour after rumour, faded away, the hopes of Charles proving a worthy Prince Charming in the romance they were set on scooping seemed wan indeed. Where, oh where was the True Princess, the heroine that he, they, and we, needed?

'The trouble was,' recalls Nigel Dempster, doyen of London gossip columnists, 'every time he appeared with a girl, I wrote a story saying that she'd had twenty-five lovers. That meant twenty-five people who'd sell their story to the *News of the World*. He had to marry a virginal person about whom there was no doubt at all.'

The insistence on purity and virginity in the jaded post-Sixties, Thatcherite Britain, with its emphasis on the 'old values' of consumerism, greed and self-interest as well as 'family', was almost subconscious at first, and sounded quaint to many when first discussed openly, but it was at the epicentre of the princess myth. The girl in question would not only have to be a suitable wife and companion for the Prince, because she would not only be 'his', but the nation's – his bride and our sacrificial lamb. Such a paragon was not easy to find.

Then one fine day in the late summer of 1980, the gossip journalist James Whitaker, most shameless and dedicated of 'royal' sleuths, was watching the bachelor prince fishing in the River Dee, near Balmoral Castle in Scotland: 'I had been standing on the river bank for about five minutes when I first noticed a flash of light,' recalls Whitaker. 'It was the giveaway that was to signal the start of the greatest romance story this century.'

The flash came from a hand mirror held by the concealed figure of nineteen-year-old Lady Diana Spencer. She was surreptitiously watching the watchers who were so soon and so inextricably to become part of her life. Who was she? 'A cunning lady,' reckoned Whitaker, a good match for him and his binoculars and lensmen. Would she also prove to be a match for the future King of England?

What would be revealed when she stopped looking through the mirror and looked down the barrel of a loaded Nikon?

That test came almost at once. Diana's name had been for some time on a list of 'possibles', albeit as an outsider, and Nigel Dempster, from one of his 'sources close to', was strongly tipped not to discount her. He thought about it, made a few calls and then wrote the whole of his Diary page in the London *Daily Mail* saying that Charles would marry her, she was The One. 'The next day,' he recalls with some exaggeration, 'there were 432 photographers at the Young England Kindergarten [the London nursery school where Diana worked as a helper]. From then on she was surrounded.'

The first pictures of Lady Diana revealed a chubby-faced teenager with a shy look, a chunky blond haircut and the general demeanour of a typical upper-class English schoolgirl. 'The girl who is bringing a smile back to the face of Prince Charles' and 'The shy girl who is winning all hearts' were typical of the headlines in September 1980.

Less than a year later, and some twenty-eight pounds lighter, the same girl was horse-drawn through the streets of London in diamonds, silk taffeta and lace, to marry the most eligible man in the world. The sun shone, the bells pealed, cameras whirred and the crowds cheered euphorically as the Prince of Wales led his new Princess to his carriage. They rode off towards his palace and in the general direction of happy-ever-after.

But where most fairy tales end, this one was only getting started. Since 'the wedding of the century', the young Princess has become so much the icon of our age that, had she not existed and been 'found', it seems that we would have had to invent her.

So 'right' did she seem from the outset that she was in effect chosen by others before Charles even knew her very well. Before the engagement she was besieged by the press to an extraordinary degree. Photographers and reporters tailed her and harassed her, but they also fell in love with her. They pushed flowers and chocolates through her letter-box and wrote her letters; one even advised her *not* to talk to him in case she lost her Prince as a result. These, her first and most loyal courtiers, were quite determined not to be cheated of their fairy story. It was not enough for the Prince of

Wales to marry a pretty girl of his choice. His bride would have to be a national dream. They had found her, he must claim her.

Since the marriage, thousands of gushing and sycophantic column inches have been written about the Princess. She has become the world's number one cover girl: not even Jackie Onassis in her heyday rivalled Diana. The film stars of the Fifties and Sixties – Monroe, Bardot, Julie Christie – did not have the pulling power of this particular blonde.

Diana started out as the girl next door. Never mind that she was a 'Lady', an earl's daughter, or that her family had very solid connections with the Royal Family – she had the *ordinary* glamour of the nice girl behind the counter at the local bank, or, indeed, the nursery teacher at the suburban school waving goodbye to children with a smile.

Her love of children and the fact that she has produced two sons in quick succession have made her not mumsy but madonna-like; her dramatic loss of weight has transformed her into a luminous, wraith-like beauty, giving her an aura of Cinderella, the girl the glass slipper fitted. The darker side to this has only served to endorse the fairy tale image: her rumoured anorexia, temper tantrums and extravagance made her seem trapped and somehow a little danger-ous, like a very beautiful, caged cat.

Regardless of what she is really like, Diana has become the strongest female image in her own country and far beyond. Girls copy her hairstyle and dress. They are held spellbound, as if by their own idealized, unattainable image in a magic mirror.

This is not a biography of the Princess of Wales, although it will inevitably retell her story, now so familiar that it has taken on a mythological quality, like the Cinderella fable to which it is so often compared. The few details we really know about Diana are lovingly repeated in print and in conversation as if the writer or speaker was handling a beautiful piece of silk or a precious piece of china. Her extraordinary and continuing appeal has made her not only the most

The first pictures revealed a chubby-faced teenager with a shy look, a chunky blond haircut, and – to the photographers' glee – no petticoat.

famous Englishwoman in the world, but also the Princess who fulfils all the requirements of the fairy tale.

This is rather a biography of her *image*, an attempt to understand its power and assess its influence for good or bad. The myth surrounding her is as old as storytelling. Why we have never grown out of it, how it both elevates and diminishes its central figure, is part of the subject of this book.

Is Diana a symbol of hope and light? Or a deluding distraction from the real, difficult world? Is she merely a spoiled rich girl dressed up, or a proper inspiration for her less exalted sisters?

Part One   The Princess

1

Mirror, Mirror

The notion of the princess sits at the centre of our collective
imagination, a glittering, inaccessible totem. Her image is half
religious, half sexual – near goddess and ultimate girl. She is everybody's and nobody's: forever shall they stare and she be fair.

The princess of fairy tales embodies female perfection at its purest
and most passive. She is vibrant and powerful – a prize – but also a
prisoner, untouchable, an icon to be worshipped. She suffers many
trials and tests of her purity and veracity. She is isolated, locked
away, poisoned, attacked by evil or jealous spirits or relatives. She
pricks her finger, falls into a coma: whatever the storyline, until the
true prince claims her, she is in constant danger, both enchanting
and enchanted. But if she survives her cruel proving, the kingdom
will be saved, the prince will rule peacefully and Happily Ever After.

A great problem is how to identify the true princess when the
world is so littered with false ones. An apparent princess may be no
more than a siren luring her victims towards rocks, a vamp, a will o'
the wisp, her purity that of Brand X, not Persil. I remember, as a
child balletomane, seeing *Swan Lake* and thinking what a dunce
Siegfried was when he couldn't *see* that Odile, the wizard's daughter
set to seduce him away from Odette, was not his true love. *Look* at
her, for heaven's sake, I wanted to shout, she's much too flashy and
she's wearing a *black* dress. But the sexual dazzle of the famous
thirty-two fouettés works its magic and the prince is distracted, not
seeing his mistake until too fatally late.

Other stories have less cruel endings, but most insist on proofs of
the princess's purity and the prince's manhood, fidelity and courage.
Both are expected to see through worldly shows of riches or beauty
to the truth.

He has to hack down briar forests and fight dragons. *She* has more curious, passive torments to endure. In 'The Princess and the Pea', a procession of impersonators sleep comfortably on the pile of mattresses with the pea concealed underneath. The true princess is identified because she is black and blue all over in the morning. Sleeping Beauty is cursed at birth so that on her sixteenth birthday – on the verge of full womanhood – the tiniest prick from a spindle sends her, and everyone else, into a hundred-year catatonic trance, until the true prince turns up with his sword and liberating kiss.

The pricked finger appears often in fairy tales. In 'Snow White' the queen pricks her finger, and when she sees the blood fall on the snow at her window, wishes that the baby she is expecting will have lips as red as blood, skin as white as snow and hair as black as ebony. Snow White is born with all these attributes but, as we know, loses her mother, and is far too beautiful for her own good. The magic mirror cannot lie when it becomes clear that she, and not her wicked stepmother, is 'the fairest of us all'. But throughout her adventures Snow White's innocence and sweetness save her again and again. Not even the poisoned apple brought by her disguised stepmother can do away with her: it only induces the inevitable coma, in which she can await a *réveil* with the amorous prince.

The sexual ramifications of this mythology are obvious. But there is a wider implication too. The perfectly matched True Prince and Princess, their virtues properly proved, will mean protection and good lives for everyone, redemption from evil. They are, in a sense, a completed circle, and a promise for the future.

We have become accustomed to the expurgated versions of these ancient stories: modern romances and mysteries deriving from them have become soft, undangerous. Sentimentality blocks out the nightmares; the gore of Grimm has been expurgated, Walt Disney has entered our souls.

In the early, pre-Perrault versions of Cinderella (it may be a story of Chinese origin) the Ugly Sisters have toes and heel amputated in attempts to cram their feet into the golden (glass came later) slipper. 'You won't need to walk any more when you are queen,' says their opportunist mother to each in turn. The unobservant prince rejects them only when he sees their stockings drenched in tell-tale blood, and returns to claim his true bride.

The dilution or expurgation of such horror is usually undertaken in the name of protecting the young, but it is in reality more likely to be parents and middle-aged people who become addicted to saccharin and sentiment, and have the strongest need to persuade themselves and others that everything in the garden is lovely, or at least safe and boring. The more affluent the society, the more there is to lose and the greater the emotional requirement for a happy ending. We, unlike the Victorians, may be able to tolerate the ending of *King Lear*; we can acknowledge the *Killing Fields*. But contemporary or futuristic allegories played out for children on video tapes and in comics are denounced as mindless and corrupting violence, as if denunciation will make the nightmares go away and we can all be left to watch *Dallas* and *Crossroads* (the down-market British equivalent) in peace.

In 1980s' Britain we are facing a cultural split of a kind far more significant than that created by our famous class system. The popular culture fed to children, particularly in the form of comics and film, is one of anger and violence and barbarity which make the Brothers Grimm look tame; that directed to adults and young women, in particular, is romantic, nostalgic and escapist.

In this context it is useful to remember, when considering the real life fairy tale of Diana, Princess of Wales, and trying to assess what 'princess' means in 1985, that every ancient golden fable had a darker, even cruel flip-side which helped give it force and meaning. And, whether we – or they – like it or not, the members of the Royal Family are part of a living, breathing fairy tale upon which we pin, and onto which we project, our hopes and fantasies.

Since the young Queen Victoria's famous resolution to be 'good' the British monarchy has both suffered and benefited from being swathed in a high moral aura of, at times, an almost sickly sanctity. The two recent Edwards – the libidinous VIIth and the abdicating VIIIth, later the Duke of Windsor – were the black sheep that proved the rule: and even today people go around sighing with relief that Charles and not Andrew is the Queen's firstborn son.

Constitutional requirements insist that the Queen and her family be above politics. But there is also a tendency, both from within the Palace and without, to insist that they be above and beyond ordinary human behaviour, which is absurd and unhealthy. The mystique and distance must be preserved, some monarchists argue, and this is obviously true up to a point. But it can, and does, endow the royals with a wooden quality, with about as much animation as a successful pop-up book that showed royal family scenes; it leads us to glorify and over-value the few banalities they do allow themselves to utter in public (Diana early on got this kind of small talk down to a fine art), and to gasp with amazement if one of their number (usually Philip or Anne) actually speaks out or expletes like a human being.

In the same manner the tiniest deviation from exemplary or programmed behaviour – any popping up too far above the parapet – is pounced on, mocked or over-glorified. Prince Andrew's womanizing, Princess Margaret's divorce, Prince Michael of Kent's beard, or Princess Michael's Nazi father, all get this sort of attention. The mystique becomes the mystique of a soap opera, not a constitutional monarchy.

There was, however, a time when a sweet moral tone suited the national mood to perfection. In post-war Britain the True Princess Elizabeth, whose early youth had been to some extent swallowed up in war, married her Prince naval lieutenant, and, within a short time, found herself Queen, heralding – so everyone agreed – a new Elizabethan age. The golden coach, the youth and much vaunted devotion to duty, together with her young family, amply compensated for her lack of film star beauty. Across the Queendom readers of women's magazines sent away for and worked embroidery samplers with a portrait of the Queen and the motto 'Faith and Truth I will Bear unto You' emblazoned on them. The coincidence of the conquest of Everest, the televising of the Coronation (the first great state occasion people witnessed in their own armchairs) enhanced the general rejoicing. Peace had indeed broken out, and old men broke down.

Winston Churchill himself is said to have had tears in his eyes at the thought of his new sovereign. 'We don't know how lucky we are to have her,' he said, having described her marriage five years earlier as 'a flash of colour on the hard road we have to travel'.

The populace seemed to appreciate their luck well enough, and the young Queen grew in popular esteem, an appropriate, comforting endorsement of everything that was respectable, dutiful and even suburban in middle-class life. She was the first of her family who, while in reality preserving her royalty and privilege, seemed to be of the people, or at least of the bourgeoisie. She seemed also to be without fault, or moral flaw. This reliability and probity were to stand her in solid stead through the years, even when the New Elizabethan Age took a somewhat wild, libertarian turn.

For the Queen was, in her quiet way, a brilliant public relations woman. She sensed that some unbending was necessary, and set about humanizing her own and her family's role. She it was who backed the BBC's *Royal Family* film of 1969, which permitted the nation to eavesdrop on a breakfast conversation at the Palace, and watch the royal sausages sizzling on a barbecue at Balmoral Castle. It was a carefully controlled, even contrived, performance, but nothing like it had ever been tried before. The walkabout, now a usual and expected part of any royal visit or tour, was also the Queen's idea. Such innovations did a great deal to hold the ground when, in the Sixties and early Seventies, it seemed that royalty, along with the other old institutions, was in eclipse: we had turned towards princesses of a different calibre and colour.

The nice Queen, the radiant Queen Mum, the Bohemian sister-princess and the rest of the entourage could not, for the moment, compete with the glamour of the new heroines of the Age of Aquarius: Jean Shrimpton, Twiggy, Jane Birkin, Julie Christie, golden girls, princesses of legs, lips and liberation. Their princes were photographers and hairdressers. David Bailey and Terence Donovan and others perpetrated a new, irresistible iconography, a sensual, grainy femininity, which was sexual, intimate and, of course, close-up. Crowns and catwalks were *out*. Women were free, explorable, exploitable, touchable: they were vulnerable and desirable, but also brave and savage. At the top of the new consumer pyramid they were unwittingly, and in the face of the burgeoning

LUNCH

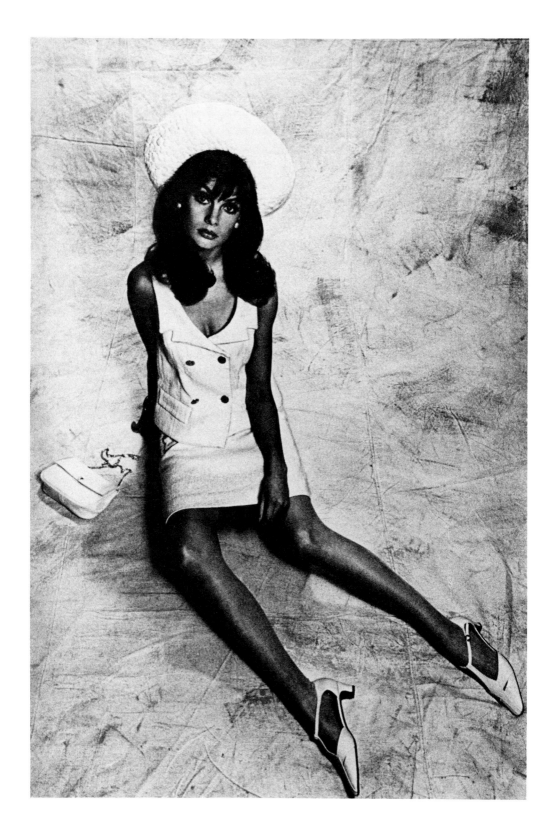

women's liberation movement, the most saleable commodity of all. Girls were the currency of the age: youth, money and success were all easy in the brave new world announced by Kennedy and Macmillan: you never had it so good, so cheap, so swinging. There was nothing to fear but fear itself. The arts flourished, barriers fell, taboos were broken.

Revolution was in the air and to be young was, if not heaven, at least heady, far out. Peace, flower power, and a sweet, anarchic idealism seemed to herald a new age. But, as at many frenetic parties, there came a moment, about three or four in the morning, when all did not seem to augur so well. People started being sick, falling asleep, drugs were passed and the mascara started to run. Had it *all* been hallucination?

Like a fairground at dawn it all suddenly seemed rather tacky. At the commercial end, brave little businesses crashed while the few survivors headed off to become pillars of the revived establishment; despair hovered over the euphoria like a vulture. By 1969 'the jitters,' as Joan Didion wrote in her retrospective essay on the Manson murders, 'were setting in.' Optimism and egalitarianism suddenly seemed to have become alienation and disenchantment. Unemployment, wars, terrorism, the nuclear stockpile. Where did the centre of dreams lie now? In a lab? At a battlefront? No longer through a wide-angle lens and up a mini-skirt.

There were some other answers. In London on the eve of the Eighties 'Back to form' was the coverline on the revamped society magazine, *Tatler*. *Tatler* may be easily dismissed as a trivial, snobby, glossy magazine, relevant only to the people it features and flatters: 'an upper class comic' the editor, Tina Brown herself called it wryly. But it holds a curious and vital place in the Diana story and in the social history of Britain in the 1980s. Brown describes what happened more neatly than anyone: 'When I took her on, *Tatler* was a dull, stodgy deb. I put her on a diet, got her into some good designer clothes, sent her to Barbara Daly to have her face done . . . she made

Jean Shrimpton, heroine of the new Sixties iconography –
a princess of legs, lips and liberation.

a very good marriage to Condé Nast [who bought the magazine in
1982] . . . and continues to live her strange life, putting on gum
boots one minute then getting on Concorde to go to a party.'

This sounds and is good, if snooty fun: what was happening
through it and behind it was the re-invention of, not just a social
whirl, but the authenticity of privilege. If the children of the rich
and established are dropping out, becoming pop stars, barmaids and
denizens of Bohemia, if chic goes down-market, then the old order
looks shaky indeed. If, however, they don taffeta and tweeds, go to
the hunt and the ball and assorted cafés blessed by society, they
represent a promise that all is essentially well. Thus *Tatler* and the
Sloane Ranger Handbook, which redefined the upper-middle classes,
brought back the twinset and pearls and revived the wilting English
rose, were enormously reassuring signals for the *ancien régime*. The
red carpet was rolled out in eager readiness for a princess.

Indeed, during 1979 there had been so much princess-hunting
that at the London *Observer* newspaper, where I was then editor of
the *Living* section, we devised a mild Christmas spoof. We picked
out an up-market secretary – a Sloane Ranger rampant called Sarah
– and had her photographed in a tiara and off-the-shoulder Hardy
Amies evening dress, and billed her as the True Princess, complete
with coat of arms and an exclusive 'interview'. A thin enough joke,
which only gained real significance later; our Sarah was in exactly
the same physical and social mould as Lady Diana, although a little
less grand: she loved animals, was a vegetarian, hated polo and
bloodsports, didn't suit her hair up and had 'that spotless purity that
convinces the masses'.

'Take her, Charles,' urged 'interviewer' Pearson Phillips, 'she's
yours. And, of course, ours.'

The True Prince himself had stopped short of throwing a ball in
the hope that Cinderella would show up, glass slippers and all. He
did not need to: concerned friends and the bride-hungry press had
conspired to find his Princess for him. At one time, close men friends
were said to have made up a book of about a dozen known virgins:
Lady Diana was about number five or six on the list. She was, at any
rate, pushed forward from within court circles; but the moment that

her shy and, at the time, well rounded face appeared under its shaggy, Sloany hairstyle the waiting hacks pounced and did not let go.

Nigel Dempster understood why the Prince followed suit: 'When Charles was exposed to all the publicity over Diana, and saw that there were no boyfriends, he realized he was on to a winner,' he says. 'He had to marry. Sharpish. A virginal girl is by definition someone between zero and nineteen. He realized that, if he let this one go, it would be a long time before he got another one. He'd be getting older and older and his possible brides would still be no more than nineteen, or even younger because girls aren't virgins that much longer. By 1990 he might have to marry a fourteen-year-old. So he saw what he had to do.'

Dempster had had the right instinct when he had studied the 'list', and listened to his informants and felt that Diana was 'the right person', at the right time. If anyone imagined that the old class and money system had been shaken by the shenanigans of the Sixties and Seventies they would have been quite wrong. By 1980 the 'Old Values' were renascent, God was in his heaven and Mrs Thatcher in Number Ten. The Queen, of course, was still on her throne. She had celebrated her Silver Jubilee; the only required redemptive stroke came when Prince Charles met the girl next door.

Until Lady Diana Spencer appeared, Prince Charles and his marriage prospects was a running but not always riveting story. There was the succession of possibles, improbables and impossibles. But Charles did not have the randy Lothario image his younger brother Andrew was later to develop. There was something anxious and almost comic about him as a wooer-prince. He frequently showed his impatience and dislike of the speculation and attention to that side of his life. It was clear, however, that he would have to marry *someone*, and that she would have to be, in his own words, right first time.

'I knew immediately that she was The One,' declared Clive James, rhymester and humorist and at one time putative court jester. The Prince seemed a little slower in the uptake but the girl herself was as sure as the press. All we know of the formal proposal is from the

Prince's own account: he 'asked her' just before she went on holiday to Australia, giving her time to think whether it might not be all 'too awful'. Diana, who later assured the world that she never had any doubts and that it was 'what she wanted', apparently responded by collapsing in a fit of girlish giggles.

Then came the engagement pictures on the lawn of Buckingham Palace. The tall, strapping Diana in her terrible turquoise Cojana suit – one of the last garments she picked off the rail in Harrods without advice – made her happiness plain. Asked if they were in love, Diana said, 'Of course'; Charles said, 'Yes, whatever "in love" may mean.'

James Whitaker, the journalist, and the Prince's biographer, Anthony Holden, followed Charles on his post-engagement trip to Australia and New Zealand. Both believe it was during that tour – and enforced absence – that the husband-to-be found out what being 'in love' meant. 'It seemed that he was falling in love with her before our very eyes,' says Holden. 'There she was splashed all over every paper and magazine. People kept saying to him, in effect, how lovely she was, that they fancied her, that he was lucky. He began to see her as we did.' Holden also recalls the excruciating moment when Charles, deplaning in New Zealand, was greeted by a line-up of 'Di look-alikes' in wigs and frilly blouses. His Royal Highness was not amused, but the clones were expressing, albeit crudely, the pulling power of Diana's image.

At the first opportunity, the future Princess showed her less shrinking and more starry side; she accompanied Charles to a poetry reading at the Goldsmiths' Hall in London wearing a strapless black taffeta dress designed by David and Elizabeth Emanuel, later to be architects of the Wedding Dress. 'That'll give 'em something to look at,' quipped the Prince.

Look? Their eyes popped. 'It was,' wrote Tina Brown in *Tatler*, 'the greatest moment of sexual theatre since Cinderella leaped out of her scullery clogs and into her glass slippers . . . she was saying, "I'm not just suitable, I'm gorgeous as well."' It has passed into Diana-lore that the Queen Mother, with whom she was staying in Clarence House at the time, ticked her off about the dress in the morning. Whatever the truth, it was certainly the first controversial

Engagement Day at Buckingham Palace: a strapping Lady Diana in one of the last
outfits she picked off the rail without professional advice.

Two studies in black taffeta: (*left*) 'shy' Di made eyes and flash-bulbs pop by baring shoulders and bosom at the Goldsmiths' Hall; (*below*) Queen Elizabeth II, nearly 30 years earlier, aroused no comment with this more demure décolletage, photographed before her Coronation.

thing Diana did and it displayed a kind of schoolgirlish mischievous daring. She seemed to be sending up her own Shy Di ruffles-and-knickerbockers look, as well as the elaborate dowdiness that the Royal Family tends to in public.

What is often forgotten, however, is that it was an extremely *conventional* dress, in spite of its décolletage. It was, what's more, almost a parody of a dress worn by the Queen, soon after her accession, without arousing any comment whatever.

Between the black bravado and the more demure ivory taffeta of her wedding day there was the beginning of a startling change in Diana. She lost close to 28 pounds in weight; her waist, by her own account, dropped from 26 inches to 21 inches. The cheekbones and the fashion model figure began to emerge. This was first remarked as she walked down the steps of St Paul's after a wedding rehearsal. 'Diana We Love You – but don't lose another pound,' crooned the *Sun* newspaper.

The voluminous fairy tale wedding dress, although it had been much taken in, seemed to swamp her. But no matter. The Wedding was the most theatrical and euphoric state occasion since the Coronation. There was not a dry eye or a silent throat by a screen or along the route. The very choice of St Paul's Cathedral, which meant a drive across town instead of round the corner to Westminster Abbey, and which has magnificent steps, was in itself dramatic. The post-nuptial kiss on the balcony of the Palace was, to the photographers, like a chance to snap the consummation; the balloons on the honeymoon carriage and the plumes in her going-away hat made Diana appear for a moment like a beautiful principal boy – prince and princess in one.

'She just can't help being nice' was the *Daily Mail's* caption for the picture of Diana blowing a farewell kiss to the Sadats as the Prince and Princess of Wales left Egypt on the way home from their honeymoon. She was glowing and nice too in the Highlands when she posed there with her husband: she said marriage was wonderful, and announced that she did not eat breakfast. This last raised a few tuts, but the girl's obvious health dispelled any anxiety. Likewise her early and bored retreat from the longueurs of the Balmoral summer court raised some sympathy and only a momentary eyebrow.

Her first official tour – correctly enough of Wales – was a triumph. The crowds sang, they pressed impossible numbers of flowers on her, children were kissed, an old man in a wheelchair wept and wouldn't let go her hand. What was she bringing them? A young pretty face? A sweet disposition? Perhaps, but there was more. The True Princess had come among them and they were claiming her as theirs: 'taking her to their hearts'.

Her husband spoke in public during the trip of 'the overwhelming effect that my dear wife has on everyone'. He was correctly identifying and witnessing a response that, among English royals, perhaps only the Queen herself, and then only at her Coronation, had ever before experienced. Diana brought hope, a sense of life; she was not part of a constitutional institution performing a role or carrying out her duties; she was the perfect endorsement of their ordinariness, one of themselves but raised to a level of celebration, adoration.

The Royal Family and the court circle had no doubt wished Charles to marry suitably and happily. Mindful of the disaster of Edward VIII and Mrs Simpson, they were determined to have a Princess of Wales with a background but not a past. Diana fitted the bill on both counts: indeed, on the second she seemed to cancel out two entire decades simply by virtue of having done nothing much in them except grow up, go to school, and (very briefly) look after children in a kindergarten.

She seemed quiet in style, domestic in inclination and pretty in a proper, English-rose way. Her full blossoming must have amazed her family and friends just as, four centuries earlier, those of the fifteen-year-old Beatrice d'Este gaped at the girl's dazzling translation from little sister to great duchess when she married Ludovico Sforza of Milan:

Energy, grandeur, verve, intelligence and beauty joined to compose around the bride – who until yesterday had been quite obscure – a magnificent show of which she was the sole heroine . . . everything she did expressed her joy in having been called to so full a life. Before the startled eyes of her mother and sister, Beatrice let go; this was her moment, and it was as if she cut herself off from all else in a frenetic drive to seize it.

In the London of 1981 the upper crust were likewise relishing a new lease of life. And Tina Brown, analyzing this revival, could write:

At last the hostesses had an excuse to rattle on the family rocks and fly in the steel bands. They all started jabbering again about a return of a smart, exclusive, well-mannered society. Watching the transformation of Lady Diana from hesitant mouse into a glittering femme fatale was a source of fun and wonderment. She was an upper-class Cinderella . . . starving herself, streaking her hair Hollywood blonde, taking her face to the best make-up artist in town . . .

And from afar off, among the cheering crowds, it seemed that the old romantic dream and the old established order had a new, living justification.

2

The Fairest of Them All

Once the True Princess has been found and proved, a second question must be asked. What is she *for*? This time fairy tales, which tend to shut down with a kiss or a wedding, are not much use as a key. The simplest answer in the present royal context seems to be that a princess is for looking at. With the exception of the Queen herself, who has a constitutional role and certain political duties to perform behind closed doors, the Royal Family has very little function when out of sight. The ever-extending House of Windsor makes appearances; its members display, reassure, and even entertain. They lend their presence: if and when they cease to do this they will become, simply, senior members of a defunct aristocracy – rich, over-dressed, over-privileged people, living in big houses.

too true!

Of course they have shown no signs of any such retreat; rather the opposite. With the exception of one or two recalcitrants, they 'work' extremely hard. In their chief requirement – to be seen – they have, like it or not, a great need of their chief public courtiers, the gentlemen and women of the press. This used to be a fairly well-ordered arrangement, with rotas and special interviews and photo-calls, and specially chosen posses of writers and photographers following the touring Queen or her representatives around. Clothes were described, handshakes were recorded. Apart from the occasional excitement of a wedding or quasi-scandal, such as Princess Margaret's doomed romance with Peter Townsend in the 1950s, it was all pretty much under control. The Press Office at the Palace fielded questions and handed out such information as was to be released, and papers loyally printed a lot of it. The foreign press were less obedient, but easy to dismiss as scandal-mongering fabricators.

quotes good!

Those were the good old, dull pre-Diana days. 'To be honest, as
far as the press were concerned it was all a bit moribund,' said Bob
Houston (an old Fleet Street veteran who once edited *Melody Maker*
and later worked for the *Sun*), editor of *Royalty*, one of the glossy
magazines spawned by Princess fever. For him, as for others, 'Diana
changed everything'. The relationship with the newspaper press has
now become one of love-hate; unprecedented Majestic appeals for
restraint have worked only briefly. The compulsive nature of
Diana's image has turned the cosy provincial matinée into a dazzling prime-time soap opera; not 'Dallas', but 'Palace'.

The real Palace, represented by the Queen's press secretary Mr
Michael Shea OBE, and his associates, attempts to brief and orches-
trate the drama, to draw a line between the footlights and the front
row of the stalls, drop a transparent safety curtain. The world's
press, on to a star of this magnitude, are not interested in such
demarcation: what they are after with Diana is what they are *not*
supposed to see. Oddly, in spite of all the wriggling through under-
growth and wielding of phallic telephoto lenses, very few of the
so-called 'intrusive' pictures of Diana have been anything but
flattering. An infamous pregnant bikini picture published in the *Sun*
and the *Star* (with the headline, 'O What a Lovely Di!') was a blurry
exception. It was in fact extremely difficult to recognize the expec-
tant lady; it was the *presence* and proximity of the photographers,
their invasion of her privacy, that caused the offence.

Some of the more seasoned members of the royal roadshow may
actually enjoy the game. That great lady of the turf, the Queen
Mother, who has never had a moment's bad press in her life, is said
to have all the Sunday papers delivered and spread before her. 'Now
let's see what they've said about us this week,' she says. James
Whitaker has fondly described the Queen Mum's endearing trick of
turning in a slow semi-circle for photographers, so that everyone can
get their picture.

So newsworthy are the Windsors now that the idea of a week or
even two consecutive days passing without a 'royal' picture appearing in at least one paper (and usually more) is unthinkable. They do
not all concern the Princess of Wales, but there is no doubt that she
is the galvanizing force.

Diana has raised princess-watching to a fever pitch, and put a princess of almost any sort way ahead of the other glamorous stereotypes: models, actresses, movie stars all give precedence to the new regality. Diana is the leader of the pack, but there is no shortage of the breed, nor of stories about them. On one day in April 1985, all the British popular national papers carried four separate princess stories, two on the front page and two inside, taking up what is normally regarded as prime news space. There was Diana 'wowing' them in Italy, Anne being a horsy good sport at Epsom, Princess Michael of Kent struggling with the shade of her Nazi ancestor, and Princess Stephanie of Monaco being forbidden by her father to model in New York. That other traditional British pin-up, the naked girl on page three, her breasts pouting hopefully, looked very much the poor relation among this glittering company.

There are two kinds of royal press coverage: the 'intrusive' reportage and photography which aim to snatch the truth, to get behind the safety curtain. Then there is the celebratory, image-making kind. They are of course linked: the first leads to the second, the second keeps the first alive and profitable. What she is *really like* is what they aim to show: how she *appears* to be is all they can ever reach.

Small wonder this long running hit series has put some strain on the leading lady. She has, after all, only one part to play – herself. No one, least of all Diana, can have guessed what she was in for when she took her fateful step, with all the boldness of an upper-class Alice, through that royal looking-glass. First, she could never get back into the nice, cosy nursery again. Not ever, not with the help of Mr Shea, nor her Prince ('Bloody peeping Toms . . . Can't you leave my wife alone for one second?') nor even of the Queen herself, who, in 1982, took the unprecedented step of offering the editors of Fleet Street tea with attendant corgis at the Palace to try to persuade them to call off their camera-hounds. 'She is not like us,' Her Majesty said. Indeed not.

Poor Diana had, in effect, married not only the Prince, but also the photographers who had, some say, helped to bring them together. They are her most loyal courtiers. They have never, except when forcibly kept out by the walls of Palace or Castle or private house, left her alone at all. And even when they are at bay, the images they have made of her are everywhere. News-stands, if she can bear to look at them, are often like halls of mirrors, reflecting back her smile, her hairstyles, her jewels, her new baby. 'There's never been a blonde like this one,' sighed one photographer, happily rewinding yet another film. 'Bigger than Streisand, bigger than the Beatles,' declared a colleague. 'She's the one we all want to look like,' said a Miss World contestant in 1984. 'The Princess of Wales is number one.'

Popular women's magazines, such as *Woman* and *Woman's Own* in Britain, report sales increased by up to 40,000 in weeks (and there have been many) when Diana appears on the cover. Bob Houston at *Royalty* admits that the success of his venture (it started as an exercise in what he cheerfully calls 'sheer opportunism' a month before the wedding, and now has a sale of some 35,000; its rival *Majesty* sells 50,000) is due to her, and that his circulation drops by up to 15 per cent if she's *not* on the front. 'She's the one that's news, the one they want to see. We often think, for heaven's sake we've had her on for the last seven months, let's try someone else. It doesn't work.'

The editor of *Paris Match* put her ahead of Bardot and Princess Caroline of Monaco; for *France Dimanche* she is 'the number one personality'. In America, Myrna Blyth of *Ladies' Home Journal*, which has a circulation of more than 5 million, declared that 'without a doubt she is the greatest media personality of the decade. She's not so available you read too much about her. She isn't trying to garner your likes and dislikes; you don't feel manipulated. The audience knows she's not doing it because she has a TV series coming up . . . And she's also very human.' One dismal American editor added, from Los Angeles, that Diana was so popular that she was ruining the business. Joan Collins, Linda Evans and even Nancy Reagan couldn't compete. 'She is a world superstar, the Beatles. She saved the House of Windsor,' says Dempster.

The other royal outsider, the undeniably glamorous Princess Michael of Kent, was, for all her beauty and brightness, left standing. As Diana's star rose, Marie-Christine's faded: she seemed *too*

Princess Michael of Kent, with bare shoulders and flowing hair, breaking 'the pain barrier' of being forty. An undoubted gift for lending her presence, but lacking the 'secret ingredient'.

like the star of a soap opera, or at least an operetta, and, even before details of her ancestry and private life were revealed, she seemed to lack innocence, the vital ingredient.

Princess Michael also suffered the slings and arrows of English xenophobic snobbery that made persistent fun of her foreign title, her accent, her first marriage and, unfairest of all, her assiduous efforts to be part of the royal roadshow. She had an undoubted gift for lending her presence and for ribbon-cutting in general, but also a gift for going slightly over the top that was gleefully reflected in every story written about her. She was too tall (nearly six feet) and 'Our Val' (short for Valkyrie) was a nickname that stuck, although it was not, as reported, the Queen who coined it. She was over-dressed – *too* many taffeta frills and flounces; she was too grand – 'more royal than we are' the Queen is reputed to have said, and just a shade too eager to 'appear'. What was more she was endlessly pleading the Kent family's 'poverty' and earned, unfairly perhaps, the image of being a royal freeloader who would, in her own words, 'go anywhere for a hot meal'. (On one occasion she even agreed to open a fast food restaurant on a motorway.) Never a story appeared without some reference to the fact that she and her husband, who in his beard and twirled moustache looked like a clone left over from a previous generation of Windsors, were not on the Civil List and that therefore all her gracious public engagements were undertaken absolutely free of charge to the public.

But the Princess was never shy of the media and constantly fed the mouths that bit her; she gave interviews, she replied to criticism, she went on *Woman's Hour* and *Desert Island Discs* and the Terry Wogan show. On her fortieth birthday she talked to Grania Forbes of the Press Association in an interview which was published with great pictorial display on a news page in the London *Times*, as well as elsewhere. She spoke of her personal feelings about being royal and about 'breaking the pain barrier of being forty': she was also photo-graphed formally with flowing hair and bare shoulders, and more domestically with her children and horses in the park of her Gloucestershire manor house. But still she appeared somehow more like a pastiche princess than the real thing.

The culmination of the veiled – and at times overt – sniping and joking came in April 1985 when it was revealed that the Wagnerian beauty's father had been a member of Hitler's élite corps, the SS. For days this juicy fact, dug up by a Marxist sociologist in a bid, so he said, to bring discredit on the House of Windsor, was a major news story. The Princess appeared on television to assure the nation that she had not known of her father's affiliation and that in any case it had all happened before she was born. Whatever the press thought, the public believed and supported her; she was not to be held accountable for her father's sin. The wave of sympathy that rolled over her accomplished something that all her eager dressing up and public appearing had not been able to do. Would it wash her across the princess barrier at last?

Then came a new calamity: rumours of an affair with a Texan oil millionaire John Ward Hunt (exquisitely enough from Dallas), ignited a scandal that blazed on the front pages for days. The Princess had disappeared to hospital to 'rest' just as the story was breaking, but soon re-emerged, looking pale, wan, and much chastened, the famous blond tresses dragged back into a grim pony-tail. Hunt vigorously denied the story, and Michael Shea was at his most outraged, declining to comment on 'sewage journalism'. A day or so later the star of this melodrama was back on form and on her husband's arm, at Wimbledon, being cheered by the crowds, who still enjoy her theatrical sense if nothing else. Hustler? Adulteress? Devoted wife and mother? Whatever mud or whitewash may be thrown at Marie-Christine, she is always larger than life, and with the beauty and histrionic nerve to enliven any episode in the royal series.

The development of Princess Anne's image provides a more interesting and telling counterpoint to that of her sister-in-law. For years the Queen's only daughter was the impossible princess from a media and public point of view. She simply would not fit the fairy tale that the press and royal fantasists were trying to script for her. Apart from the fact that she could hold neither her temper nor her tongue, she didn't *look* right. She was striking and powerful in appearance, but that was all wrong. Great efforts were made, not least by the lady herself. She wore a lot of stylish hats with huge brims. Norman Parkinson, the most sugary of portraitists, shot her in over-the-top soft romantic focus, wearing silk chiffon, tiaras and even white fur, always making the most of her marvellous hair. She appeared on the cover of *Vogue* (which Diana, at time of writing, has not); but it was never enough to dilute the fierce intelligent stare, or conceal the wide, often sulky-looking mouth. 'She *is* beautiful,' protested Parkinson when people accused him of 'making' her so. Perhaps, but more in the style of Elizabeth I than Cinderella.

What is more, she set herself extraordinary standards of personal achievement. To become a horsewoman of Olympic standard she had to take what she was doing very seriously. Anne does not simply *appear*, she *competes*. She has talked about what it feels like trying to win an event, coming up to a jump only to see 'all those eyes and cameras just waiting for me to fall off . . . I realize that the horse is the only person who doesn't know I'm royal.' Perhaps that is why she remains so devoted to the beasts. Certainly the best picture 'Parks' ever took of her was on horseback, galloping into the distance with hair flowing loose.

'Born to terrify' wrote Jeffrey Bernard, the *Spectator* columnist, and there is some truth in his irony. 'The only one of the whole lot with any brains,' said a former escort, and this may also be true.

The rehabilitation of her image, which she may have cared about more than she pretended, came about through her own hard and committed work for the Save the Children Fund. No lady bountiful in a pretty frock to be wheeled out for a ball or some other fund-raising occasion, Anne went striding through the most dangerous and distressing of famine and disease-ridden areas in the Third World, genuinely finding out what was happening there and talking lucidly and intelligently about it when she got back home. She emerged, if not as a royal Mother Teresa, at least as a grown-up, independent-minded woman, plugged in to the world outside the royal hothouse.

She also shows formidable energy, undertaking more public en-gagements – some 250 a year – than any other member of the Royal Family apart from the Queen, and a great sense of humour. As well

Princess Anne, in white furs and diamonds for the cover of *Vogue*,
but beautiful in the manner of Elizabeth I rather than Cinderella.

Anne in Somalia: no lady bountiful in a pretty frock to be wheeled out for a ball or fund-raising occasion.

as out-wisecracking Terry Wogan on his television chat show, she stepped in to save gold medallist Daley Thompson when his ebullient, rather risqué jokes about wanting to marry her might have taken the gloss off his Olympic triumph in Los Angeles in 1984. The Princess silenced a pompous chorus decrying his insolence and lèse-majesté by issuing a public statement to the effect that anyone who had taken what Thompson had said seriously was an idiot.

What Anne still will not do is inhabit a glass case, and, although rumours of antagonism between herself and her sister-in-law are largely fabrication, their styles are quite different, and Anne's impatience with the Diana roadshow is all too apparent. At Christmas 1984 she went rabbit shooting rather than join the adoring family gathering round the crib of Prince Harry. At least three gleeful national British newspapers thought that 'Anne Snubs Di' was the most important news story of the day. Both Princesses dismiss tales of discord impatiently. 'It was a genuine previous engagement,' said Anne and pointed out that her children had been there making enough noise to compensate for her absence. (If there was a falling-out on this occasion, it was between brother and sister, not the sisters-in-law.)

In fact the two women have complementary, rather than conflicting images. If Anne 'does', Diana 'is'. The Princess of Wales's life is in itself an event: the smallest and most ordinary action or occasion is a justification for her existence, and fuel for public interest. Much the same weight is given to a change of hairstyle, a family squabble, or a new baby.

It was prophetic that Earl Spencer so assiduously kept photograph albums recording every stage of his youngest daughter's life and growth. Since she met her prince, life has been a photo-call. Her love affair with the camera – or perhaps the camera's love affair with her – has transformed her from a 'nice', suitable teenager into the prime female image of her time: part icon, part Barbie Doll, the greatest English rose ever.

Her career has been a photographer's bonanza. They snap her from in front, behind, the side. At times the cameras appear to be carving her up for our easier digestion. They snap her ankles, her neck, her hair. And she, in a sense, has learned her own image from looking at the results. And these days, far from cracking under the strain, she has gained the upper hand. The new shimmering *sexy* Diana, who appeared at a London charity gala early in 1985 and managed to outshine Joan Collins with a figure-hugging and revealing creation by Bruce Oldfield, had truly left knickerbockers behind. 'Princess Di-nasty' and 'Di-namite!' shrieked the headlines.

She refuses, however, to play Barbie Doll obediently all the time. Setting out on her tour of Italy in the spring of 1985 she was billed as Britain's 'fashion ambassadress', and at the same time criticized sharply for reputedly spending £80,000 on a new wardrobe to fill the role. The Princess retorted in the only way she could by appearing at her first gala occasion of the tour wearing an old and not particularly stunning evening dress. Later she relented and brought out the new spangled dresses and bow-tied suits.

It is not, of course, only magazines and newspapers that enshrine and project the image of the Princess. Glossy picture books recording her fashions (but not always naming her designers), her foreign tours, her babies, offer portable galleries of portraits for the faithful. Many feature the work of Tim Graham who has made a career out of photographing the Princess and is now a favourite with her. Her approval of his pictures – which far outnumber those more formal shots by Lords Snowdon and Lichfield – show the value of constant press photography to the new royals. 'Harassment' is only part of the story.

When it comes to books it does not seem to matter how often the same pictures appear: repetition seems to reinforce rather than reduce her appeal, and a new volume will often start off with some of the old favourites from the early days of the marriage or even before. The books can also offer an almost cinematic quality, presenting three or four frames in sequence, obviously taken only seconds apart.

The most inventive in this genre must surely be *The Pop Up Book of the Royal Family*, a best-seller on both sides of the Atlantic in 1984. It was a masterpiece in loyal paper engineering, with text by no less than Patrick Montague-Smith, former editor of *Debrett's*

Peerage and Baronetage. Diana features large; indeed there would probably have been no such book without her. The balcony kiss is on the cover and again, in animation, inside. In a family group with Charles and baby William, the Princess looms forward at the tug of a small paper flap. And so on. The cover blurb offers the book as a 'souvenir' or a 'memento': 'Surely never before has a family been so often photographed and painted – so seldom does one see a new image. These "pop-up" scenes supply several.'

Like most female members of the Royal Family Diana is not expected to speak very much, although she has developed a happy line in chat for the walkabouts people love and flock to. She has recently taken to advising fans to warm up with a stiff whisky or gin-and-tonic when they get home, and she always discusses babies readily. 'Nobody told me it would be like this,' she groaned of her morning sickness. But the less she says the better it is, the more her magic is conserved. 'I can't stop looking at her,' said a five-year-old at the time of the wedding. This compulsive viewability has been there from the beginning, but it has also been developed and exploited by the fashion industry, the press, and by the Princess herself.

Her prettiness, or beauty, is only an ingredient of her irresistibility. When she first appeared she won hearts with her extreme youth, her almost pudgy face and her inexpensive, but up-market schoolgirl's clothes – knickerbockers and frills, cotton skirts, simple jewellery like the D necklace in her first photographs. She looked like everybody's favourite daughter.

Her first attempts at centre-stage dressing had a mixed reception. The engagement suit was a rather touching attempt by someone very young to be formal and smart. The frightful outfits she wore to Ascot that year (under advice, it is said, from a lady-in-waiting) were fortunately outshone by her own personality and evident happiness. The effect was got-up, fussy; at this stage she could have seemed like a promising apprentice in the royal school of over-dressed dowdiness.

The black taffeta dress was different, the sartorial version of making a face at the photographers who had besieged her for so long. The fact that it didn't suit her at all didn't matter: it was a stunt.

Prudence Glynn, former fashion editor of the London *Times*, made bold to express disapproval in an article in an *International Herald Tribune* supplement to mark the Paris collections in spring 1981. Glynn roundly said that the Princess-to-be needed some better advice, and that, among other things, a strapless dress at dinner 'made one look as if seated in a bath'. These frank words were not deemed tactful and soon afterwards Glynn's column in *The Times* was dropped.

All the same, also very soon afterwards, Diana began her course in fashion under the watchful eye of Anna Harvey, Grace Coddington and others at *Vogue*.

Diana had always adored shopping. The engagement saw the last of the days when she could do it alone, with time to wander into a friend's office and throw off her shoes and eat a Mars bar to gather energy between stores. In those days she patronized, in common with girls of her age group and background, Laura Ashley, Benetton, Fiorucci; she was a South Molton Street, Harvey Nichols, Harrods customer, an habitué of what the press calls the 'Tiara Triangle' between Knightsbridge and Sloane Square.

What is a princess for? A princess is for looking at, and she looks best, or best satisfies our imaginative demands of her, when she is dressed up. There has been, predictably, among the envious gasping and gaping at Diana's clothes, some waspish sniping about her extravagance, especially during the first extraordinary year and a half of her marriage. She was 'A right royal shopaholic' who allegedly bought 50 ballgowns and 200 day dresses and suits in a year, and clocked up a bill of £1,500 a week. But in this, as in her choice of 'the biggest ring on the tray' that Garrards sent round to help her select an engagement ring, she was doing no more than behaving as most of her admirers and contemporaries wanted a princess to do. Her evident delight in her new and priceless collection of jewellery adds to this. 'I'm a very rich woman now,' she is said to have declared when presented with the fabulous sapphires and diamonds which were a wedding gift from Saudi Arabia.

Gasping at such luxury from afar is, on the whole, a gasp of admiration and pleasure, although closer to home her rather more parsimonious husband is said to have been appalled by her early spending levels. Once again there is a parallel with Beatrice D'Este who, like Diana, had grown up in fairly simple style: after *her* marriage 'everyone found her 84 new dresses, heavily embroidered with gold thread, jewels and pearls, excessive. They hung in a great room that, as her mother observed with graceful irony, resembled a sacristy hung with all the canonicals.'

There have been similar stories of bulging wardrobes at High-grove and queues of Harrods vans outside Kensington Palace. But, as the *Sun* said supportively, '£30,000 a year on clothes may be a fortune for the rest of us, but it is "well within her means".' The icon must be pure and remote; the Barbie Doll must have the best the world can offer.

There is another, more commercial, point. The Princess of Wales has provided what was a rather flagging British fashion industry with an unprecedented boost. 'She has given Britain the most exciting fashion image in the world,' says one of her favourite designers, David Sassoon. Even during pregnancy she contrived to dazzle. For two years running readers of *Woman* magazine voted her the country's best dressed woman. Both Sassoon and *Woman* might have added the words 'classic' or 'conventional' to their praise: the real 'excitement' of British fashion was, and is, at the wild, street end of the market. Diana breathed new life into a more genteel, coffee-morning and cocktails style of dress.

But unlike older members of the Royal Family who, on the whole, display a kind of benevolent unconcern for clothes and patronize one or two designers each (the Queen gives her couturiers turns at the great occasions, rather as if they were photographers on rota), Diana shops around. The Princess, says the Palace, 'works hard' on her public wardrobe and increasingly chooses her own designs. But there are, as we shall see, critics who feel she was caught between the fuddy-duddiness of court requirements and tradition, and the eager exploitativeness of *Vogue* and the rag trade who could not look such a marvellous clothes-horse in the mouth.

It was on the Australian tour in 1983 that the extent of her diffuse
'patronage' became clear. As Nicholas Coleridge bitchily reported in
Harpers & Queen (*Vogue*'s closest rival) she carted Down Under,
packed in 90 trunks, clothes by no fewer than 21 designers. And
here, too, her princessly image was established. Coleridge declared it
to be 'very pretty, very sensible, utterly Sloany – but not innova-
tive'. For the most part, he was right, although he omitted to include
the hit dress of the tour – Haachi's shimmering off-one-shoulder
creation that made her look more like the Little Mermaid than
Cinderella. It also, along with one or two of the more casual outfits
she wore around the same time, had a touch of the Sue Ellens about
it. This aura was aided by the increasingly skilled, and increasingly
obviously skilled, use of make-up. Her adviser here was and is
Barbara Daly: black eyeliner *inside* the eyelashes, grey outside.

Sloany? Perhaps. Glamorous? Of course. But, tiaras apart, the
Princess was dressing to the aspirations of young women in banks
and building societies and shops and offices, up and down the country. They might not be able to afford a Bruce Oldfield or a Gina
Fratini, but they would find clothes in the same language, if not the
same fabrics, in Richard Shops, Next, Miss Selfridge and other high
street chains. Their hairdresser would be, and was, pleased to copy
the hairstyle. Jewellery? Who needs *real* diamonds? Fake jewellery
has never been more attractive or decorative. Like her mother-in-
law before her, the Princess had hit and revitalized the true style of
suburbia.

And, in so doing, she illustrated a curious cultural phenomenon.
After a decade and a half of everyone dressing as seventeen-year-
olds, we had returned to a middle-aged formality and norm. In the
Fifties young middle-class women dressed like their mothers and
grandmothers: twinsets, pearls, seamed stockings, high heels,
tailored suits and perms. In the Sixties and Seventies mothers
dressed like their daughters: mini-skirts, cotton T-shirts with no
bra, blue jeans. Formality was a white frilly blouse and a long cotton
skirt or some sort of ethnic robe. The return of important, competitive taffeta and its surrogates for teenagers also heralded a return to
formality in everyday dress: proper frocks were back.

Crowning glory: when Diana presented Harry to the nation, the blond
hair formed a seraphic cloud around her well made-up eyes.

I am writing here, of course, about the majority: the women that editors refer to patronizingly as 'mainstream'. But the mainstream is what is carrying us all along: the colourful extremities, the punks and post punks, fade daily. The 'Casuals' who patronize the shops favoured by Sloanes buy good quality stuff: leather, pure wool, tweed. The hard edges visible in *The Face*, the New Restoration brocades and powder in *Harpers & Queen* are only the sophisticated, outré extensions of this new traditionalism.

The Princessly hair has been the crowning glory of her image. One of the most endearing things about her, at first glance, was that she did not have hair that looked 'done'. It was cropped into a thick blond cap in the manner of many of her clan. It was the easiest aspect of her looks to copy: in fact, it was already a fairly popular style in current use. Diana maintained it for nearly three years. She wore tiaras but never headscarves; above all she wore hats. These concoctions, many of them pill-box-and-veil creations by John Boyd, have been widely criticized. 'She is not a hat person,' re-marked Michael Roberts in the *Sunday Times* after her first Ascot series. Nevertheless, she persisted; the hats were part of the new formality-chic, while the hair was a trademark of her youth.

Gradually, however, during her second pregnancy the Princess let her hair grow into a softer style and streaked it ever blonder. Presenting her second son, Prince Harry, to the nation (as repre-sented by the gaggle of photographers waiting outside St Mary's Hospital) the blond hair formed a seraphic cloud around her well made-up eyes. The pictures taken that day are far more vibrant and symbolic of what the Princess means to people – an 'ordinary' if radiant mother carrying her new son from a hospital – than are the rather stilted, even scary, studio pictures by Snowdon, taken two weeks later. In these Diana wore white satin, her eyes seemed bloodshot, her expression posed, affected – an icon trying too hard.

A short while later, at the State Opening of Parliament, she went the whole way. The Princess put her hair up. The occasion itself always rates coverage. It is, aside from the Coronation, the best public sight of the constitutional monarchy in action: the only chance people have to see their monarch, flanked by her children, actually sitting on a throne wearing her crown. Even if she is wearing spectacles under the Black Prince's ruby and enunciating Mrs Thatcher's plans to demolish the Greater London Council, it is an impressive sight.

This time the twenty-three-year-old Princess of Wales took the not unremarkable step of scraping her hair up under her tiara in a kind of GI bride's roll. She was, as she must have known she would be, photographed from every angle. A couple of weeks of amazing newspaper nonsense ensued. The *Daily Mail* invited readers' views and were deluged, mainly by letters saying that the style made her look too old, or too like other royalty – again, notice, claiming her as one of 'us', not 'them'.

What was going on? An identity crisis? Vanity? Experiment? Was she practising being Queen? A fashion editor informed me that she 'had it from three hairdressers' that the Queen would abdicate in 1985 and that's what lay behind the change. The story of her switch from Mr Kevin to Mr Richard in one hairdressing salon – 'the fall of a royal favourite' – provided some bitchy copy. Such was the furore over the Rape of the Look that *The Times* was moved to write a leader deriding the antics of the 'popular' papers. 'The Princess must have been left wondering whether it was her hair or theirs,' it thundered, rightly quoting the *Daily Express* headline – 'Is she still our Di?' – as going to the heart of the matter. The leader continued, 'The general complaint seems to be that the new style makes her look less like the girl next door and more like a princess. But the Princess is in fact a princess, and it can be assumed that all the girls next door who so assiduously looked like her will be looking like princesses too, as soon as they can make an appointment with their own stylists.' *The Times* thought it would be a 'sad paradox if the Princess took seriously the uproar from those who regard her image as their property and resorted to the most obvious line of retreat by making herself in fact the "royal clone" she is accused of becoming.'

The Princess obviously understands her relationship with her subjects better than *The Times* does. She returned to the soft, pretty style they like, and carried on smiling. For, if the earlier rumoured anorexia threat hinted at an unwillingness to grow up on her part, the hair sensation showed that we do not want her to age, or take on queenliness, just yet. The icon should not move without permission. The link between the living image and its idolators is a delicate one.

However, by Christmas 1984, the Princess had succeeded in a more gentle graduation to maturity. In the film – a kind of royal home video – of the christening party for Prince Harry and in the subsequent pictures, again by Lord Snowdon, Diana appeared with some of the grand manner of a Queen Mary mixed with the misty fabulous beauty of a Thirties' film star. Never mind that her voice, as she chatted to her two-year-old son, still had a hesitant, little-girl quality: the Princess of Wales had arrived. The image of Shy Di had been erased at last.

Part Two   The Press

3

Diana the Hunted

The triumphant wedding procession of the Prince and Princess of Wales, in July 1981, wound down the hill from the grey-and-gold domed pile of St Paul's Cathedral, straight into what the couple might be forgiven for regarding as enemy territory.

It was somehow exquisitely appropriate that the first few minutes of their married life should be spent driving up Fleet Street, avenue of shame and shamelessness, shock-horror and tit-'n'-bum exclusives, and, of late, hub of the Diana pursuit-and-promotion business. She had had, before her engagement, a frightful time of it with her journo-huntsmen, but on the wedding day at least they seemed well under control, tamed by the barriers of royal ceremony and crowd control. It was, for a moment, as if the barbarians had been subdued, and their victorious lady was doing a lap of honour as she rolled back towards the safety of another grey-and-gold edifice, and the protection of her courtiers and spokespersons, the royal buffers of the Buckingham Palace press office.

Mr Michael Shea, the Queen's press secretary, and Mr Victor Chapman, who 'looks after' the Prince and Princess of Wales, occupy what must be among the poshest offices in London. Approached by long corridors, along red carpets and past marble busts of ancestral royals, they sit among dark mahogany furniture overlooked by gloomy portraits. Mr Chapman's lofty windows give a good view of the Palace gardens where he says he can sometimes see the Queen playing with her dogs and grandchildren of whom she is inordinately fond. Always at the ready, on hangers behind their panelled doors, suits of morning clothes into which, like courtly Supermen, they can spring if summoned to the Presence.

Diana's most loyal courtiers: it soon became apparent to her and everyone else that photographers were to be part and parcel of her marriage.

Back at the Cathedral end of the processional route the hacks with whom Shea and Chapman alternately skirmish and treat, work and drink in much more cramped and seedy surroundings, where they congregate, speculate, process and publish, and – with luck – may grow rich and famous on the proceeds.

The relationship between press and palace is a volatile but productive one, based on love-hate, with a certain amount of mischief and scorn thrown in from the Fleet Street end, countered by pomposity and evasion from the Palace corner. For Shea and his staff are there to shield as well as promote, and often find themselves fielding stories that have originated from some other unofficial 'source close to' the family. Dempster, for example, says he never speaks to the Palace; his information comes from franker, more reliable, and of course anonymous, contacts. Harry Arnold of the *Sun*, one of the most constant and prolific Diana reporters, may occasionally, out of courtesy, call Shea in advance, if he is about to publish a story upon which the press secretary may be called to comment. Arnold has scant sympathy for the Royal Family's beleaguerment: 'There are many things in life you can be born, and there are a lot worse things than being born a prince or princess.' He also believes that they are what they are twenty-four hours a day and should accept that; and he reckons that they manipulate press coverage far more than people realize. 'It's an art form with them,' he says.

It was the Queen herself who mastered this art form first. 'I have to be seen to be believed,' she said neatly and accurately. And so she instigated the royal walkabout, killing off forever the old, stiff, magic lantern show aspect of royal appearances and visits. She understood that in a video age, ceremony and pageantry were not enough. People needed to know that the Royal Family were not just symbols and ciphers, but that they were real, like thee and me. So Her Majesty, along with the rest of the previously untouchable royals, started to press the flesh like politicians on a campaign trail. This was not only exciting for those who got physically close outside the Town Hall or new hospital, but it was good, lively television, bringing the presences into the living room more effectively than any amount of pomp and circumstance could do. It is a little sad, perhaps, that the Queen, for all her acute publicity sense, has come to realize that, however adored she may be, she doesn't quite have the overwhelming appeal of Diana, or even of her own mother: 'If it were Mummy, they would *all* be cheering,' she is said to have remarked drily on a subdued outing. And she was much annoyed that even 'my own television station' (the BBC) failed to cover a visit to Sweden. Nevertheless, she permitted the Royal Family film, defrosted the Christmas broadcast, taking the chance to show her family at work and play in a safe, stage-managed way. Her Majesty is said to revere Diana for what she has done, and been the first to encourage her to stay young and unstuffy, and reach out to people in a way that the Monarch herself cannot.

All of this broke the royal ice, and the days when the Palace press office operated as a rather sedate and discreet limb of the royal household, issuing anodyne circulars and statements, gazetting engagements, marriages and births, and (at least until the denial of Princess Anne's imminent engagement) being believed, or organizing rotas, photo-calls and tours, were numbered.

There had, of course, been crises before, the most monumental being the Abdication of Edward VIII in 1936, but in those days the press were a cowed and manageable lot. Witness their willingness to remain silent about Mrs Wallis Simpson for so long, and, perhaps even more revealing, the fact that Edward VIII's main complaint about the invasion of his privacy was that there was a persistent sketch artist hanging about in the Mall hoping to catch a glimpse upon which he could base a saleable drawing. What would he have thought of James Whitaker's portable bag of instant disguises, or Ken Lennox's probing telephoto lens? Post-war, Princess Margaret's doomed romance with Peter Townsend was painful but quickly over. But since the advent of megastar Princess of Wales the press secretaries have had to transform themselves into the impresarios of a show destined, as reporter James Whitaker says happily, 'to run and run, right into the twenty-first century'. Which should see him and his cronies through nicely. The new style of court life established by the Princess, with the obvious connivance of her Prince, has for the first time brought the shadowy backstage courtiers into the press

spotlight. From the outset, there were stories about Diana being
high-handed and arbitrarily sacking Charles's long-term staff. One
of them, a valet, even sold his story saying so. The most significant
departure was that of Edward Adeane, the Prince's private secretary.
He did not sell his story to anyone, although again Diana was
blamed. It appears, however, that it was exasperation with Charles's
changed attitudes towards his duties that caused Adeane to give up,
and at time of writing a search for his successor had proved fruitless.

It is clear that these stories of imperious staff dismissals and difficulties hurt Diana more than anything else. She took the unprecedented step of seeking out James Whitaker at one public occasion
and telling him that they were untrue: 'I don't just sack people.' In
fact, the problems may have much more to do with the Prince than
his Princess.

Charles, since acquiring his Princess and thereby, in a sense, his
adult freedom, appears radically to have changed his perception of
being a Prince. He has cut his schedule to a handful of engagements
a month. This is partly so that he can be with his adored children as
much as possible, but it is also his recognition that Diana is the one
for whom the crowds turn out. 'You'll have to make do with me,' is
how he tends to deal with his side of the walkabout crowd. Or, as he
told a posse of trainee priests in Rome, 'Don't worry, your beauty
queen will be along in a minute.'

But, while increasingly allowing her to do her magical appearing
act alone, Charles has been busy establishing a new, slightly eccen-
tric sort of court. Almost, indeed, cultivating an alternative style of
Windsorism. For this he has gained enthusiastic respect from quar-
ters not usually interested in royalty at all. His spirited and public
defence of classical, as opposed to modern, architecture, his concern
for the countryside and interest in organic farming, not to mention
his vegetarianism, all strike a deep chord in the national conserva-
tionist sub-conscious. He is the hero of the New Georgians (who
care about great houses and fancy dress) and the Young Fogeys (who
care about everything that happened before they were born and wear
their grandfather's tweed suits to prove it), and all groups of ultra-
traditional, anti-modern intellectuals.

All very well; but this cranky side, his interest in spiritualism and natural medicine, reflexology and biofeedback, are not at all reassuring to the stiff upper lips and collars of Whitehall. Nor is his taste in gurus: his devotion to the philosopher Laurens van der Post, with attendant talk of mystical and religious experiences in Africa, and his liking for the remarkable Dr Miriam Rothschild, authority on fleas and other parasites, and perpetrator of a seed mix of weeds and wild flowers known as 'farmers nightmare', which Charles has been cheerfully sowing round Highgrove House, is not easy for a conventional courtier to swallow, let alone serve.

What's more, no one from diplomatic circles, it seems, wishes to work for the increasingly reclusive husband of a superstar who is increasingly showing that she understands her own power to get and do what she wants.

The Princess has changed the press too, and transformed the lives and status of royal reporters. Court correspondents have taken on some of the flash and fizz of showbiz writers. In the Eighties in Britain, Diana has been the biggest booster of circulation and bylines, apart from Bingo and the Falklands War. And, in spite of internal difficulties, she was also a boon to the Palace promoters. Shea, the urbane, charming, former diplomat, writer of thrillers and television scripts, may not, any more than the Princess herself, have bargained for such continuing and obsessive interest, or a story that press and public were going to want so much. 'How long can this go on?' asked a dismayed Princess when she saw her appeal grow, rather than decline, after marriage. 'Until your daughter is as old as you are now,' said Prince Charles shrewdly. As Mr Whitaker said, it will run and run.

The Queen, in her loosening-up policy, had in a way concentrated on allowing the press and people close enough to hear what the Royal Family had to *say*, to prove that they were not just icons to be looked at, and revered or reviled according to your view. There were an increasing number of rather stilted interviews with top royals, such as the pre-marital encounter with Princess Anne, in which One acquitted Oneself as well as might be expected. Anne later told another interviewer that, given the choice, she'd rather have been a

long-distance truck-driver. Prince Philip and Prince Charles have
been more than ready to speak at length about their favourite causes,
and Princess Michael has been willing to talk to reporters, over a hot
meal or even the telephone, at any time. All a far cry from the days
when Princess Marina of Kent ticked off her new son-in-law Angus
Ogilvy for referring to Princess Alexandra as 'my wife' and not as
'Her Royal Highness'. Distance and mystery must be maintained,
she argued, or royalty was finished.

But in a sense it has been Diana's success, rather than the Queen's
careful gradualist policy, that has set the lesser members of the
family free to speak for themselves. Diana's has been essentially a
picture show; she has such a plausible and all embracing royal image
that the others can all afford to relax and speak up a bit. She not only
looks, but she looks marvellous, and, however intrusive and mad-
dening her photographers have been, they have served her very
well. The difference between the Princess of Wales and the star of a
television soap opera is that Diana is not an actress, she is herself
playing herself.

Nigel Dempster, who sees the Diana story as a photographic one,
reckons that Diana has learned a great deal about how to develop,
simply from studying her own image. She has, not as some other
commentators think, suffered an identity crisis, but chameleon-like
moved on with the times and the storyline. 'I think she knows that
she's real because I think she is very simple,' says Dempster. 'She
will never grow up because she knows nothing about nothing. But
she is brilliant at what she does. People want silly chatter from her,
they don't want intellectual debate.'

In accounts of her early relationship with the press, Diana is
usually presented as the completely innocent victim, agreeing to
pictures without knowing what effect they would have, saying
things that were open to misinterpretation or even the correct
interpretation, which was worse. There were indeed times when her
situation became insufferable, and others when she was tricked, as
with the famous sun-behind-the-skirt picture on her very first
photo-call. But, with hindsight she looks, on the whole, like a lady
with a genius for public relations, who knew exactly what she was

doing and how to manipulate and mislead the hounds baying at her door when she so chose.

Whitaker saw her as a 'worthy opponent' at the outset. Her control, her politeness, her skill at avoiding them, when she wanted to, are all evidence that she, not they, was in charge of the situation. The photographers and hacks say that they forced Charles into marriage. This may well be so; but Diana did a clever job of forcing them to force him. By her very shyness and blushing non-denials she encouraged the rumours and whipped up a storm and a siege through which she could quite reasonably call out for help and rescue like a damsel in distress.

Even the infamous Royal Train story run by the *Sunday Mirror* which alleged that the sweet and virginal Lady Di had spent a night of passion on board a train, in a siding in Wiltshire, rebounded to her advantage. The story was untrue, but, regardless of that now undisputed fact, the editor of the paper, used to public delight when a sacred cow is toppled, miscalculated totally on this occasion. Not only did he get it wrong, but the public did not *want* to hear such a story about their new heroine, even if it were true. Diana emerged not only smear-free but more virginal than ever.

The tussle about publicity *after* the wedding, and after that triumphal progress up Fleet Street, was different. From afar, it looked as if, having handled things so well, and having got herself home and dry on the Palace side of the fence, the girl was safe from harassment at last; but it soon became apparent to her and to everyone else that the photographers were to be part and parcel of her marriage, rather like the courtiers of old who hung out in the king's bed-chamber, never leaving him alone for a minute.

It was the sense that she could not even walk out of her front door in the country to shop for sweets that caused the first big crisis between Palace and paparazzi. This happened during the siege of Highgrove House, the couple's Gloucestershire home which is clearly visible from the main road below to the naked eye and telephoto lens. Because the Princess was pregnant at the time, the Palace, in the shape of Mr Shea again, took unprecedented action. National newspaper editors were invited to that special press conference, followed by a meeting with the Queen herself, and asked to call off their hounds. Shea and HM correctly assessed the appeal of such an invitation: the people who run the rough trade of newspapers affect to despise royalty as chocolate-box people, putting them in the paper only as decoration or titillation, but on this occasion they galloped to answer the summons, well-titillated themselves. Frank Giles, then editor of the *Sunday Times* and an avowed monarchist and courtier manqué, spent half his main editorial conference that week recounting the joys of the visit, chief among which had been an exchange between Her Majesty and the editor of the *News of the World*, who had suggested a simple answer to Diana's shopping problem. Couldn't she send a servant? 'That's an incredibly pompous thing to say,' said Queen Elizabeth II, who runs a household of some six hundred menials. Everyone laughed at the *NoW*'s discomfiture, but the question had been fair enough. The Royal Family, as Harry Arnold pointed out, can't have it both ways, unless editors permit it.

The only editor who did *not* run to the Palace was Kelvin Mac-Kenzie of the *Sun*, who pleaded a previous engagement with his proprietor. 'I must remember to call and congratulate him,' growled Rupert Murdoch. 'Ridiculous nonsense. What the hell do they expect, buying a house five hundred yards from the main road.' Murdoch himself can show his courtly side when he chooses, as when he attended a party at Hatchard's bookshop, at which the Queen and Prince Philip were present.

The heat did reduce a little after this, but a year later it was back at inferno pitch on the ski-slopes of Liechtenstein. This was probably the worst moment between the image and her makers. She hid her face and sulked, Charles got angry with her, and angrier with the press, who in the end had only one answer. 'Come on, love, we are not trying to pull your teeth out.' Again Shea put on his exasperated hat and stormed at the press, with dark hints of a permanent damage to the relationship between the future King and Queen and the nation's communication industry. But it was a little like threatening a divorce when you have six children, no money and nowhere else to go. It also ignored the fact that Fleet Street accounted for a minority of the snow-slope cameras. The Princess was the pearl in the world's oyster by this time.

Fences were repaired later by a series of lunches, stage-managed by Shea, at which the Prince and Princess met the editors two by two. The *Guardian*'s Peter Preston, most cryptic of editors, heading the least slavishly royalist of papers, asked the couple how the species had impressed them. There was a lot of laughing between the couple and then Diana said that well, you know, the fellow everyone says is so awful at the *Sunday Times*, they had rather liked *him*.

Shea has been called everything from 'a brilliant diplomat' to 'a paid liar', which in some Fleet Street minds amounts to much the same thing. The strange bind in which he functions was perfectly exposed when, in 1982, an American journalist working for *McCalls* and *Woman* magazines published, with full attribution, an interview she had had with Shea and Victor Chapman on the subject of the state of the Royal Marriage. It had revealed nothing detrimental – little more than that, yes, they did sometimes have rows, ate light meals and that the Princess had found royal life hard to adjust to at first; but it broke the unwritten 'rule' that these Palace spokesmen should never be heard to speak, that their briefings be unattributable, not seeming to come from anywhere near the horse's mouth, but handed down from on high, as if to Moses on the Mount. A year or so later the *Observer* columnist Sue Arnold went on the tour of Italy where she began to understand 'the Humpty Dumpty logic of Royal tours. When Prince Charles shakes you by the hand, looks you straight in the eye and tells you something legal, decent, honest and even funny, you can't report it. When you crouch behind a pillar eavesdropping . . . you can report it.'

Oddly, one of the sources of the difficulty that the Princess has had with the press is that she has liked and understood what it has done for her only too well and, consciously or unconsciously, spurred their interest. From the outset she acknowledged their physical presence and had no truck with the imaginary glass wall the others use to protect themselves. As recently as her 1985 trip to Italy she was able, after struggling through an Italian greeting, to turn to the cameras and say sharply to her men, 'Work that one out.' But if she

Di versus Dynasty: the new, sexy image of the Princess has raised temperatures in Fleet Street, and upstaged Joan Collins.

So has Jayne Fincher

knows how to flirt, she also knows how to sulk: James Whitaker has watched her spend ninety-nine per cent of the time at a public engagement with her back to the cameras, or looking at the ground. The fact that she is, as Tim Graham has said, so marvellously photogenic has put her in control. She only has to look round for a moment, as she did on the steps of St Mary's Hospital after Harry's birth, for the right picture to be possible.

'She has brought sex and glamour to the Royal Family,' says Dempster. 'She has uplifted it. She's glamorous, sexy and she's posh, posher than the Queen. The Spencers had Mary Queen of Scots staying in their house. Diana's a wonderful creature and nobody's ever going to find her otherwise, no one's ever going to interview her or get anything foolish out of her. Charles has done himself an enormous amount of good. Until she bolts. Of course she *can't* bolt. But if she does it will be a great, great story . . .'

The new sexy image of the Princess has raised the temperatures of Fleet Street veterans in 1985. There has been much imaginative speculation about how and when the Princess might or might not take a lover and, naturally, how they might catch her at it. They are gleefully aware of the squeeze they have her in, surrounded as she is with servants who might talk and photographers who might snap. They have watched her dancing all evening at the party where she upstaged Joan Collins, and they *know* . . . They will wait, and, inevitably, they hope, they will see.

4

The Language of Sugar and Spite

The turn of phrase and tone of voice that tend to overcome anyone addressing either the person or the subject of the Princess of Wales, in print or in the flesh, is revealing.

If the writer or speaker is being celebratory, paying court, or otherwise hoping to catch the lady's eye or ear, the style may be so shot through with sycophancy and sweet nothings that it is 'pretty amazing' (to use Diana's own immortal phrase to describe her first impression of Charles) that she has not long ago expired from saccharin poisoning. Platitudes and clichés meld in a wondering, gasping, almost orgasmic prose, which is at the same time tinged with possessiveness and cosy over-familiarity.

This mode is used to record the most banal of her sayings and doings, even at times to scold her a little for her lapses, real or imagined, while all the time paying tribute to her elevated ordinariness. In some newspapers and magazines you may find the written version of the silly expression that comes over people's faces when the Princess (or any member of the Royal Family, for that matter) enters a room, or strays near them on a walkabout. It is a kind of 'in-the-presence-of' fixed grin, which appears to combine with an instant evacuation of the brain and a tongue-tied inability to say anything sensible. This can even affect self-declared anti-royalists, or republicans such as Rupert Murdoch. When the Queen visited *The Times* offices in London, to mark the centenary in 1985, the proprietor was seen beaming in an uncharacteristically inane fashion all over his own back page.

If the writer or speaker, however, is more distanced from the white heat of the presence and is merely gossiping and speculating,

he or she will tend to a self-important 'mark my words' style, and
refer to 'Charles' and 'Diana', 'Anne' and 'Mark', etc. as if they were
the folk that dwelt on the hill, or in the next street. It is the same
sort of fantasy that is applied to the villainies of J.R., the agonies of
Sue Ellen, the machinations of Alexis Carrington/Colby in *Dallas*
and *Dynasty*. Soap opera gossip is an easy kind of conversation to
start; royal gossip is the easiest, anywhere, in any company. It is
also the easiest copy to write, but may be laced with prurience and
ill-will – the kind of 'salacious voyeurism' complained of by English
feminist writers Ros Coward and Diana Simmonds in an article on
the press and the Princess in the *New Statesman* in 1984. The
notion that the perfect girl may be not so perfect after all can unleash
an almost lascivious, spiteful glee. This may, as in the anorexia
'scare', be disguised as concern for her welfare: in the same way that
a scandal sheet may pose as a moral bulldog while exposing the
scandalous vagaries of actresses and bishops.

The most striking thing about the wordage and tittle-tattle woven
round the Princess is that the vast majority of it is of the former
favourable and flattering variety. At first, quite appropriately, she
was accorded special indulgence because of her youth and sweetness
and because of her surprise value. The delighted astonishment that
someone so 'nice', so 'fresh' and so 'natural' and, above all, so
'*suitable*' should somehow have been thrown up out of the writhing,
sullied mass of modern humanity seemed incredible, unlikely luck.
That early approbation developed into a doting obsessiveness.
Women in the street (including traffic wardens, if James Whitaker is
to be believed) spoke of her adoringly, girls wistfully, longing to be
like her. And all the time, of course, their interest is wound up and
kept going by the sugary prose that is loyally pumped into the
column inches of papers and periodicals like so much molten
toffee.

Does it soothe? Comfort? Give delight and hurt not? If we can
contribute to our lovely Princess's happiness, can we add to our
own? It may be so. Certainly there has developed in the public print
an almost superstitious desire not to give offence. The increasing
dignity and experience of the lady, not to mention her increasing

family, has led to greater respect. Perhaps it is because she has, clearly, weathered the second round of princessly tests and trials. During her courtship it was siege with wishful writing about secret assignations on trains, etc.; after her marriage it was rumours of rows, tantrums, anorexia and a potential breakdown. Now, as a mother of two and a more and more assiduous fulfiller of engagements, she is well cemented to her pedestal and there is less and less taste for trying to topple her (except, perhaps, in the wishful thinking of gossip columnists). Her future role is referred to more frequently, as if to hurry along the plot.

There is more, if covert, reference to her adult sexuality and glamour. But, with the pictures of Prince Harry, came phrases such as 'new maturity', 'firmness and serenity' and 'fulfilled and happy mother' and, to crown it all, 'very much our future Queen'.

Not long after that, in December 1984, Catherine Stott was writing in the London *Sunday Telegraph*. 'At twenty-three the Princess is the epitome of a beautiful English woman, with her thoroughbred features and perilously long and slender racehorse legs. The cheekbones have become Garboesque in their definition, the nose has a hint of imperiousness.' Note, please, how the word 'perilous' is introduced, presumably to evoke some residual emotional vulnerability, rather than any actual physical wonkiness.

In newspapers, the further down-market you gallop, the soggier the going, although little can, these days, match the slush of the wedding coverage. In July 1981 the world's press rushed to London and stretched every known language to its limits in an effort to encapsulate the magic day. On the native front, the *Daily Express* might have been expected to take a good middlebrow line. Certainly it was a day when clichés came into their own, and the best one of all was caught in the picture of the day: 'Sealed with a Loving Kiss' proclaimed the *Express* over the balcony shot on its front page. 'The tender moment that crowned the happiest day.' And on the back was a picture of 'the radiant bride who stole everybody's heart'. ('Radiant?' snapped Veronica Horwell in the *Sunday Times* later, 'makes the lady sound like the element in a gas fire.')

Inside the paper the columnist Jean Rook, self-styled 'First Lady of Fleet Street', was herself pictured outside St Paul's in her wedding finery – a big hat and a fur stole – looking as far as possible like a genuine wedding guest. Her 'colour' piece describing the ceremony is a classic of its genre and, even as Princess prose goes, well over the top:

> She rose to the occasion like the 365ft dome of St Paul's. She glittered like the tear in her bridegroom's eye. Her confidence shone like the thousands of sparkling sequins in her 25ft veil. It blazed with joy from her tiara-bright eyes. It burned like the TV arc lamps, like the lectern's 5ft winged eagle. Like the polished rows of . . .

And so on and on, all measurements carefully included.

Rook did insert a human line of pre-Princessly nerves by quoting Diana as saying that she was so-nervous-she-didn't-know-what-to-do. But of course she *did* know, and gave Rook the chance to describe her as 'one ivory cream thrill, with a bouquet like a dripping, cooling waterfall'.

During her translation from Lady into Princess her courage was 'as lofty as the thrilling, echoing dome, her head now higher than the vaulting sound of *Pomp and Circumstance* as she swept down the aisle on Prince Charles's arm. The too-often bowed neck was swan-like as the towering feathers of the Gentlemen at Arms. It rose from a plunging mass of frills like the last thrilling sounds of the House-hold Trumpets.'

The morning after the wedding, when this soaring prose appeared, was the first on which Diana could be correctly addressed as Princess, the word we had all been waiting for. It rolled off the typewriters and tongues of the hacks and into the consciousness of the crowd, to emphasize that an elevation, a sacrifice almost, had taken place to create Her Royal Highness. 'Carnival for the Fairy Princess' was the *Daily Express* headline for the main report of the day. And their leader was headed simply 'Our Princess'.

The paper had also hired Robert Lacey, author of *Majesty*, a biography of the Queen which had helped get the new-style royal show on the road, to write a 'think' piece. He quoted the late Lord Mountbatten's warning against sentimentality in relation to the

The Wedding Day kiss on the Palace balcony, while press and populace frothed in a soda-stream of sugary babble.

Reversed, damn it.

monarchy, and underlined the *authenticity* of the jubilation. No
one, he pointed out, was waving a flag by decree.

The leader-writer called Diana 'a breath of fresh air'; 'our
youngest and latest ambassadress, she will project a thoroughly
modern image of Britain throughout the world – bang up-to-date
but with all the old traditional values.' And those old traditional
values had, indeed, never looked so young. Diana was, the *Express*
reminded us, the 'third lady in the land' and 'all our lives, not just
the Prince's, will be the happier for Princess Diana's infectious
smile. His great catch is our national asset.' Thus, from day one, the
Princess of Wales was proclaimed a national treasure.

Of course, long before the wedding fever erupted, a Di industry
was already flourishing; it was not long afterwards that the first
coffee table – or at least cake-trolley – books began to appear. The
books are pictorial creations; they record every move, every flinch,
every smile. They give access to the inaccessible, rather in the
manner of space probe shots of the surface of the planet Venus. You
can look, but you can't touch. If, indeed, any ordinary mortal *does*
touch, that is news of a shocking kind. '*Naughty*!' hollered the *Sun*
in its splash (its main lead story) the day after a loyal but over-
enthusiastic subject (a boilermaker, as it happened) stole a kiss. Di,
according to the *Sun*, 'ticked him off' saying, 'You are supposed to
shake hands.' The man's apology had something to do with the fact
that he couldn't resist her. Schoolboys and children fare better, and a
cancer patient once claimed that his pain had left him after the
Princess had touched him. The idea that the touch of a king – or a
queen – is curative is as old as monarchy itself.

Most of the Dianarama books have text that is little more than
caption material, and certain words crop up over and over again.
'Sheer' is a favourite: the Princess's 'sheer' ease, her 'sheer' elegance
and her 'sheer' loveliness, 'shine' through her 'modesty', 'youth',
and anything else about her that can be designated as translucent.
Sometimes there is an attempt to create retrospective tension, a hint
of danger. The writer will note that the crowds *nearly* got out of
control, that the Princess *might* have tripped, or slipped, or caught
her heel . . .

One of the first and most 'sheerly' elegant of the books was also the one with the best title. *Princess* by Robert Lacey was designed by Michael Rand, art director of the *Sunday Times Magazine* and designer of Rupert Murdoch's company reports. It is contrived as a classy, fairy tale storybook, with decorated capital letters and the text printed on pale yellow paper.

At the outset Lacey acknowledges that there is a dimension of the story he is *not* going to tackle. Diana is too young to merit a biography, and he will not attempt 'to pursue too far the eccentricities of the human psyche that lead us to single out a few of our fellow human beings like her and set them apart and then to bestow upon them affection and loyalty and respect which no rational process of thought can either justify or destroy.'

So, putting analysis aside, he contents himself with the announcement that she is 'everybody's sweetheart, a national pin up of the nicest sort. And she is only just twenty-one!' 'Nice' was an early Diana catch-word, one which set her apart from the fast, the bad and the glamorous, and indeed from the whole of the preceding generation of girls with their allegedly wild, even promiscuous ways. 'Nice' was undeniably what Diana was, and it set her up as a proper example from the beginning. (The exclamation mark – 'screamer' in journalese – is a stylistic device that would have made Lacey wince in earlier days.)

He did not, however, shrink from reminding us that the 'blood had to be renewed', nor from endorsing Diana's welcome in 'a world grown sick of rebels and ravers'. Already Shy Di was emerging as a high priestess of reaction: 'The qualities of moderation so generally admired in the Royal Family were alive and well and had been living in Earl's Court in the custody of someone so young and pretty and eminently *balanced*. She had been tried and tested in the previous months. She had stood the test.'

Lacey quotes the Wedding Dress Emanuels in verbal frills worthy of their frocks: 'She must emerge from her carriage like a butterfly breaking out of its chrysalis.' (Obviously neither of them has ever seen a butterfly breaking out of its chrysalis. It is a remarkable, but hardly a speedy or graceful process and is performed without benefit of footman.) He also quotes *Woman's Own*, according to whom Diana, poor lady, was a 'piece of unseasoned wood ready to be fashioned into a stately and polished figurehead'. Lacey hoped they were wrong, but resorted to the time-honoured fairy tale formula at the end of his book, nevertheless. 'The glass slipper was missing, but the youngest sister from a broken home did get the gown, the glass coach and, of course, the charming prince. The wand was waved by us because we wanted her to carry and keep alive our hopes and dreams and fantasies.'

Not everyone wanted to goggle and gawp and gush. From within her own world emerged gossipy jibes: 'Lady Sly', 'Super-Sloane'. In the *Tatler*, Tina Brown cracked a joke: 'All the others beached Wales; Lady Diana saved him.'

But for the most part the press and populace frothed in a soda stream of sugary babble. Small wonder that it soon palled – with the new Princess if with no one else – and we began to get the flip-side of the story. Our heroine was feeling 'the strain', she was 'lonely and bored', or again 'lonely and bewildered'. She was also displaying 'iron will' and was, in private, not a near-dumb blonde beauty, but a 'shouter' and 'real screamer'. She herself was quoted, or misquoted, as telling her new husband that she felt 'like a princess in an ivory tower'.

Once again it was Nigel Dempster who blew the whistle first. He had a story of fairy princess-into-fishwife, in which Diana, isolated at Highgrove, had objected, to the point of screaming out of a bedroom window at him, to her husband endlessly going off hunting and leaving her alone. She had become, he said in an interview on television, 'a fiend' and 'a monster'.

There were a few lumberingly gallant journalistic attempts to come to her rescue, but the image of a highly strung, wayward, selfish girl grew. It was also the beginning of the image of Diana as a victim, trapped and terrified by what she had brought on herself. There were tales of her refusing gifts from the Queen, and sight of

Diana the lonely? For a time, the image of a highly-strung, wayward girl, trapped in an ivory tower, took over; the fairy became a fiend.

her playing up on public occasions. She freaked out on the ski-slopes and she turned up late for the annual royal 'must', the Remembrance service at the Albert Hall in London. Suddenly the sugar-and-spice language of the press turned sour. Diana was 'a spoiled brat', according to Jean Rook, author of the dome-hovering prose quoted above. There were other vicious tags: 'Sulky Di', 'Difficult', 'Highly Strung', 'Wilful', 'Spoilsport', a 'Right Madam', 'Diana the Dictator', 'Shopaholic'. She was also, in this part of the plot, anorexic, a disease not of slimmers, but of those refusing to grow up.

In the end, however, the explosion of bad press did no more than give edge to the story, made the conversations at the bus stops or in the coffee breaks more exciting. Any girl imagining herself into the Palace with her prince could no doubt also imagine herself into the claustrophobia and restrictions, as well as the clothes and jewels. The papers, having had their story, followed it up by rushing to her defence and to explain and interpret the crisis. What they wrote, particularly a series by Unity Hall in the *News of the World*, might have been a sketchy biography of any young woman's first years of marriage. Isolation, loss of old friends, lack of freedom, which no amount of love and adulation could instantly cure, were all too credible. Plus, in the Princess's case, the great public appetite for her in her most perfect, smiling and 'happy' manifestations. They wanted to see her smile, but they also quite relished hearing about her off-stage reactions. One of the most abiding images of the young Princess evoked at this time is of the girl wandering around High-grove with only her Sony Walkman for company, or dancing and working out for hours to 'unwind' after public appearances.

It was not, in any case, long before the superlatives and the sugar were back. Diana was 'Princess Superstar', she was an 'Ice Cool Satin Doll', 'A Dazzler', 'Stunning', 'Singleminded'. Above all she was still 'Ours'. The possessive had not been dropped; she had not got away. The second pregnancy confirmed her as a perfect example of young, healthy motherhood. There was less talk of morning sickness, she scarcely appeared to gain weight until the very end, when the *Sun* could coo over a picture of her that she was 'So Pregnant, So Proud, So Lovely'.

So, the Princess is stunning, glowing and radiant. She emanates warmth, life itself, perhaps, hope of it, certainly. She is also – thanks to the anorexia rumours and two pregnancies – delicate, precious. Sometimes she is written about as if we require her to be no more than the walking and well-clad endorsement of the banal, the shallow and the unambiguous. At others she accrues an almost witchy power.

The nature of that power is interesting. Her real strength is as a crowd and press puller: people want to see her, touch her, imagine they know her. She is, as Diana Simmonds wrote in her jaunty and irreverent book, *Princess Di – The National Dish*, an object of desire. Diana herself may have *actual* power only to shift a penful of photographers back twenty paces from her aircraft and wreck their chances of a good picture that day, or cut down the list for a photo-call. Otherwise, she is in a plot she can't change much. The Royal Family is now very dependent on the Diana Factor, and they seem to know it. Were she to vanish in the flash of a bulb, the House of Windsor would seem a drab series indeed. We, press and people, starmakers and children of a video age, have found the heroine we want, and have loaded on to 'our Princess' the whole responsibility of continuing a real life Dynasty.

What has evolved to maintain her is a new, or revised style of courtly language. Through the pages of books, magazines and newspapers the adoring public has access to its icon. A writer in the *Sunday Times* suggested last year that the monarchy would have to 'go showbiz or go to the wall'. But Diana is not just a branch of the entertainment industry. Whatever razzmatazz may attend her progress she is, or is being presented as, the perfect example of a 'new' kind of womanhood – which of course turns out to be the oldest as well. She, and we, have concocted a recipe which includes purity, beauty, motherhood, sweet femininity, with the modern essential ingredient, slenderness, thrown in.

When Diana was a kindergarten teacher living in obscurity in Earl's Court and for a time after she graduated to the Court of St James, she was said to have eaten 'more chocolate and sweeties than were good for her'. Her new thinness and those 'perilous' racehorse legs suggest that she has grown out of that addiction. She has, however, been force-fed by the media on sugar of a much more addictive and potentially pernicious kind. It may undermine and decay rather than shore up the old, once solidly comforting, institution.

Even the most royalist of newspaper editors are prone to this weakness. Frank Giles, when editor of the *Sunday Times*, refused to commission a major piece on the Princess phenomenon because, among other things, it might 'sound anti'. When William was expected, he declared that he would, if the baby was a boy, commission William Rees-Mogg to write a 'pompous open letter on the Review Front' (the paper's main features space); if it was 'a gel' he wanted 'some nappies and goo' on the woman's page.

William was born and Rees-Mogg gave rein to his pomposity. But goo, with or without nappies, has been much more the diet Diana has been used to receiving from her most loyal subjects.

Marina Warner, when working on her book on the Virgin Mary, recalls that, even while she could still stand in the nave of Notre-Dame in Paris deeply moved by the love and worship she felt, she held fast to her 'new intimations that in the very celebration of the perfect human woman, both humanity and women were subtly denigrated'. This paradox is, albeit to a less exalted degree, also at the centre of the Diana cult, or factor, or worship (all words frequently used to label her 'phenomenon').

Catherine Stott, at the end of her retrospective piece on Diana, noted that in newspaper cuttings libraries the wallet marked 'c' for 'criticism' was the slimmest of all, and, in the same paragraph, looked forward to watching the Princess develop further. The danger may be that she is permitted only a two-dimensional development; that the press and the Palace, whose own 'unattributable' catch-phrases such as 'caring' and 'working mother' and 'extremely fit' ricochet round magazine and newspaper reports like too much suet in the pudding, will wind her in a web, not of lies, but of stultifying clichés.

Part Three   The Projection

5

Happy Ever After

Nicolla sat next to Lady Diana Spencer under a hairdryer the day before the engagement was announced. She remembers her giggling and blushing, and recalls knowing that this was the famous Lady Di. The next day her father brought home the evening paper with the pictures of the happy couple in the grounds of Buckingham Palace, and Nicolla, thrilled to have been within a blow-dry of history, cut them out and pasted them in her diary. She was thirteen, the Princess-to-be was nineteen.

So began a lasting devotion of a kind that Diana has inspired in girls and young women growing up in her shadow – although not many take their loyalty to such lengths. After the engagement pictures, Nicolla cut out the pictures of Diana in her sensational black evening dress, and then more and more, until it was clear a diary wouldn't hold them all. So she started a scrapbook, then another and another. By the spring of 1985 she had 64 volumes piled up in her bedroom of her parents' house in Dorking, Surrey. She has filled them carefully with pictures, but also notes, and comments. One day, she says, she may present them to her heroine; or she may keep them as an heirloom for her daughters or granddaughters.

Nicolla goes to Princess Anne's old boarding school, Benenden, in Kent. In term-time she competes with friends to get to the newspapers with her scissors first; in the holidays she spends all the £45 a month clothes' allowance that her father gives her on travelling to see her Princess in the flesh, and buying papers and magazines to add to her current scrapbook. If Diana appears on the cover of a magazine she buys two of that issue, one to cut and one to keep. She would like, she says, to be a lady-in-waiting, and in a sense she is one already.

She once waited for more than five hours in the cold outside the British Museum in London. The Princess, who has come to recognize her disciple, had waved at her on the way in; Nicolla just had a feeling that if Diana saw her again on the way out she might stop the car and speak to her, and accept her posy of flowers. But at the last minute a policewoman stood in the way: 'I think she thought I was going to throw the flowers at the car,' said Nicolla. 'I was so disappointed.'

On other occasions she has been luckier, and the Princess has taken notice and stopped to chat.

I always call out to her . . . people say, how can you, she's a princess, but I do. It's not that I don't respect her, it's just that in a way I feel I know her, she's still an ordinary person, the one I saw in the hairdressers. I asked her if she remembered me, and she said, 'How could I forget?' Another time she asked me who was paying me to follow her around. I said no one, I paid for myself and she smiled and told me not to waste too much of my money on her.

To achieve such moments Nicolla has to be on site early, along with the photographers and hacks, and she enjoys rubbing shoulders with them and joining in the backchat that goes on during the long wait. She also takes her own pictures, and says that Tim Graham has been especially kind and helpful to her. Watching him get out of his BMW one day she knew that he had done pretty well out of the Princess, but Nicolla reckons he deserves it because his pictures are so good and, anyway, 'she wouldn't be what she is without the photographers.'

Nicolla says she continues to spend (she would never say waste) her money as she does because she admires the way Diana has made the Royal Family so much more real and informal. Before, they were so high above and really out of touch, she thinks. 'I love the way she sticks up for what she wants; I like the remarks she makes, the little jokes. And she is the only one who *always* does a walkabout. I love the clothes she wears; she looks good in everything,

Street touchability: the Princess, snapped by her loyal fan Nicolla Hewitt, pressing the flesh on a walkabout.

she has such a thin waist.' Nicolla would not, however, buy the same clothes herself and she can see some poignancy and restrictions in the princessly situation: 'I think it is a shame she has had to grow up so fast. I wonder if when she is forty she might not look back and wish she had had her life for longer.'

Nicolla, who said she was really serious about wanting to be a lady-in-waiting, also has other more realistic ambitions: she wants to be a presenter on television.

Rosie is thirteen, goes to a London comprehensive school and wants to be an artist. She has a very different view of the Princess. 'I used to really like her at first but she's boring now; she just has become a Dallas woman and dresses as if she was fifty.'

Rosie herself is in the process of inventing her own style: which owes nothing to Diana, nor, she hopes, to anyone else. She has close-cropped gelled and spiked hair which makes her look like an astonished elf; the style, she maintains, was *not* copied, but achieved by telling her rather smart Kensington hairdresser what she wanted. 'I don't read magazines, I like to be original.' The influence of *The Face* and street culture is, however, obvious. Rosie listens to Sixties music – Eric Clapton, the Rolling Stones – and has a huge picture of Marilyn Monroe on her wall: 'Not because she is sexy, but because she is a wonderful actress.' *Some Like It Hot* is her favourite movie.

Not all Rosie's friends would agree with her about Diana. The 'Casuals', the tribe of kids who wear ultra-conventional designer clothes with all kinds of rituals about how the labels and logos should be displayed (or not displayed), admire her a lot. At the time of our talk, Rosie said the Casuals were into permed hair and diamante brooches and patent leather shoes with laces which, she felt, was all pretty boring. Rosie, who, if she belonged to any group, would have called herself a Trendy, sticks to 'American' clothes – jeans, sweatshirts and sneakers or baseball boots. She never wears dresses and only sometimes a skirt. She used to like Benetton clothes but thinks they have gone too flowery and *pink*. She doesn't like Wham! or Michael Jackson ('all their songs sound the same'), and, though her father buys her *Just Seventeen* magazine, she doesn't read it ('I haven't the heart to tell him') preferring a bizarre satirical

Street credibility: the young, sulky, wised-up
fashion faces of the Eighties.

comic called the *Fabulous Furry Freak Brothers and Fat Freddy's Cat*.

She and her friends are into parties and music and CND. They talk about the possibility of war a lot and are very, very frightened about it, she says. No, the Princess of Wales could do nothing to dispel that anxiety. Rosie planned to spend some of her summer at a West Country peace camp; certainly not royal watching, although she really likes Prince Charles. She is happy about being a girl and feels on very equal terms with boys: she'd like to marry and have babies one day (not, like her Casual friends, at seventeen), but won't have a man bossing her around, she's sure about that.

Nicolla and Rosie are at opposing and extreme ends of the scale of reaction to Diana. To discover how girls in general viewed both the real Princess and themselves I devised a questionnaire which was sent to different kinds of schools in different parts of England. It was answered by 50 girls between the ages of thirteen and seventeen.

Geography appeared to make little or no difference to the replies which, with a few exceptions, had an almost uncanny uniformity about them. Private schools produced fuller and sometimes jokier answers ('It's Diana's job to protect Charles from the royal corgis'); the girls seemed to have a clearer idea of an 'establishment' in society, and consequently of their own place within it. The most comprehending answers about feminism came from a London comprehensive: they were the only ones who used phrases such as 'equal rights'.

A number of questions required the respondents to compose their own short answers rather than simply tick a choice from a list. The important query 'What do you think is the main duty or function of a princess in 1984/85? (If you think there is none, say so)' drew many total blanks from the comprehensive school girls. One or two did take the trouble to write, 'Don't know'. Some who did answer were preoccupied with her duty to the Third World, birth control, and representing Britain abroad: 'I think the Princess should set a good public example about helping the Third World. She should not have more children than she expects others to have'; 'She should represent England in other countries'. They also thought she should be a figurehead and inspiration at home: 'Her function is to be seen by the public and to be seen helping people in need'; 'To keep up tradition and maintain an image people can relate to'; 'To be responsible for attending social functions and helping charities and being the figureheads'. Her healing powers were obliquely recognized: many girls featured 'visiting hospitals' as her main duty.

The comprehensive school girls were more concerned with Diana's public-spiritedness and community duties. The private school girls emphasized her private role: she should, they reckoned, 'Set a standard and generally support her husband at all times'; her duty was 'To produce an heir and be a good wife, supporting her husband and to endeavour to carry out her own enterprise too'; 'To promote good relations with her husband and provide an heir'; 'To impress the public and country and support her husband. To be happy'.

Others concentrated on her appearance. She had a duty to 'look nice and act as royalty should'; 'to have babies and look good for photographers' and 'to be a focus for the media'.

The most interesting thing revealed by the survey was a clear link between the girls' hopes for their own futures, and their perception of the Princess. They were given a choice of adjectives and asked to choose one that would, in their view, best sum her up. The alternatives were Beautiful, Snooty, Vain, Sulky, Happy, Ordinary, Lucky. If none of these fitted they were invited to suggest a word of their own. An overwhelming majority – more than eighty per cent – chose 'Happy', with 'Ordinary' and 'Lucky' vying for a very poor second place. (Additions to the list included 'Brave' and 'Sweet'.)

The next question asked the girls to state their own greatest ambition in life. Again the vast majority said simply, 'To be happy', or composed an answer which included the word: they wanted to be 'happy and rich' or 'rich and famous and happy' or be 'happily married'. The choice of the word 'happy' linked all groups and ages. The girls perceived the Princess as being 'happy', and 'happy' is what they aspired to be themselves, sometimes in combination with wealth or security, sometimes with love and marriage.

O-level candidates from the Midlands did use the word 'job' or

'good jobs' in their replies about ambition, often conjoined to notions of independence. 'I want to get a good job, buy a dog and live
on my own'; 'I want to gain a profession so I can support myself and
not have to rely on a male to support me'. A-level students at a
private school hoped for good careers, but very few specific ambitions were stated. 'Actress or hairdresser', 'journalist and author',
'graphic designer' were some exceptions. One girl wanted 'to be well
known in a model sort of way', another declared that she wanted to
get into Sandhurst. There was one aspiring chartered accountant,
but no engineers, doctors or lawyers among the replies.

Fame and money meant more to the private school girls; the
desire to be 'a good wife and mother' was evinced by comprehensive
school respondents; one said she 'wanted never to have to worry
where the next meal was coming from'.

There was a strange confusion about the meaning of the word
'feminist'. In answer to the question, 'What does the word feminist
conjure up to you?' a startling number seemed to think it was a
synonym for feminine: 'Someone who gets her hair permed'; 'A
tall, beautiful, blonde woman dressed in beautiful clothes and acting
very ladylike'; 'Someone who's feminine and a bit of a poser';
'Someone who's dressed well and sits behind a desk' were all
answers from fourteen-to-fifteen-year-olds.

Of those who did understand the question, the answers tended to
a simple statement such as 'Someone who believes in equal rights for
men and women'; others were more opinionated: 'Over-
enthusiastic, headstrong women'; 'Greenham Common cow';
'Someone who strongly believes women are God's gift to men';
'Fanatical'. The phrase 'over the top' recurred and often came from
girls who said they liked or approved of some feminist ideas. 'They
go too far sometimes'; 'I'd like to rely on my husband'; 'They go
over the top and picture an annoying butch person who wants to do
away with chivalry altogether . . .'

At the same time, most of the girls revealed that they admired the
Princess; some admitted to envying her. They claimed, on the
whole, not to have been influenced by Diana's clothes or hairstyle,
but one or two said that, like Nicolla, they had 'kept a scrapbook' of

her pictures. Even those who were 'annoyed' with themselves for doing it said they couldn't resist reading stories or articles about her or looking at pictures in magazines.

The nicest thing about being her, they tended to agree, would be the travel involved, and also 'not having to worry about money or getting a job'. The two worst aspects would be, predictably, being photographed constantly, and not having freedom to follow her own interests. So, although the girls are well able to perceive the restrictions in the Princess's position, they long, all the same, for its benefits – security, protection and glamour.

They were vaguely or even sharply afraid of being dependent, but saw money and material benefits as a possible compensation for this. Being famous, or 'well known' might be the best form of independence, certainly the best protection against the anonymity that can overcome a woman after marriage.

Diana, one or two of them reckoned as they handed me back their forms, had it all, except freedom and privacy. They were fascinated, even inspired by her, but would not really like to change places.

Just before the wedding, *Harpers & Queen* magazine published Lady Diana's Lament ('With love and good wishes from the H&Q piper') which was a little too true to be funny.

Goodbye to hearing the doorbell ring and running to find out
Goodbye to looking as bad as you feel
Goodbye to thinking you are liked for yourself
Goodbye to garlic and risking your health
Goodbye to private ownership of your own body.

The girls were never going to be asked for such sacrifices of self, but they clearly understood the dilemma, and universally condemned the press as 'too nosey and pestering'.

Whatever their hopes or fears for the future, all the girls I spoke to, or who filled in questionnaires had something to say about Diana's appearance. Their comments were nearly all admiring, although they tended not to like her hats and thought that her more recent ultra-glamorous *Dynasty* image was less appealing than her earlier, more girlish style. Even when they, like Nicolla, loved her clothes, they denied being actually influenced by her or wanting to copy her directly. They mainly, like the five-year-old I quoted earlier, just couldn't help looking at her, riveted by her combination of physical and personal qualities, her ordinariness overlaid by privilege and status.

'You can never,' the Duchess of Windsor is often quoted as having said, 'be too thin or too rich.' Diana has proved that you can never be too young, beautiful, thin or rich. Her thinness marks her out perhaps more than anything as a physical heroine of her time; the sudden way in which she shed her teenage heft when she met her Prince served to endorse the notion that love is as much to do with slenderness as tenderness. I had expected the schoolgirls to relate to her figure but when they did it was often to remark that she was 'too thin'. Perhaps it is too soon for them, perhaps they have read all the warnings about anorexia and heeded them. Certainly it seems to be slightly older women, the Princess's exact contemporaries and above, who gaze most admiringly and enviously at her magical, size ten, clothes-horse figure.

When she first came on the scene, there were all kinds of cloning games played in magazines and at airports with girls playing Shy Di from under heavy fringes and above frilly blouses. But the most thorough-going 'double' who copied the Princess was Julie Wooldridge, a young married woman from Essex, who had spent most of her life nicknamed Porky – until she discovered her likeness to the new Princess, that is. People would stare at her face and then look away from her large, 14 stone (196 lbs) body. Julie worked hard to achieve all-over resemblance.

'Every photo of HRH was like looking in a mirror at the figure I could become . . . once the vision hits you you have to make it real.' She did, by losing 4½ stone (63 lbs) and buying, four sizes smaller than before, 'the kind of smart suit' that Diana wears. She was bowed to by boys on a tube train, chased and photographed by Japanese tourists, and then appeared in her local paper and was

Off-the-shoulder, off-the-peg imitation: Julie Wooldridge (*far right*)
worked hard to achieve all over resemblance to her famous mirror image.

launched as a professional look-alike with modelling sessions and appearances and television commercials in Britain and abroad. Eventually after some yo-yoing between fat and thin, Julie was named 'Slimmer of the Year' by *Slimming* magazine. They dressed her up in copies of the Princess's clothes – including the famous Haachi dress which exposed one shoulder and one leg – and photographed her in full colour on the cover and across six pages of the magazine, billed as HRH, Her Radiant Happiness.

Julie, who was twenty-five when this transformation came over her, says she is eternally grateful to the Princess for showing her her other self. 'She is my inspiration.' She is also touched by reactions she herself inspires. Even when people know quite well she *isn't* the real Princess, they will smile and walk up and shake her hand and ask for her autograph. 'Little children approach me with flowers. It's as if, by being nice to me, they are showing the warmth with which the Princess is regarded.'

What the Princess's image seems to do is to reassure; she makes it all look possible, and it is only when she goes too far over the top into super-glitzy attire that she gets any adverse criticism from her young and contemporary admirers. They prefer her to seem a little shy and vulnerable, like themselves, like to be reminded that a woman's main responsibility is to take control over her looks and body and make the best of them. The Princess did have anorexic tendencies; subduing your body by starving it is often the only kind of power a young, frustrated girl can exercise, and this is what Diana did. But, however near the edge she came in that unhappy period after the birth of her first child, she has now achieved a balance and sits perched on the pinnacle of the health, fitness and body-consciousness boom that produced the 1980s' ideal of female beauty and strength.

6

The Prince, The Wimp and The Wardrobe

Diana's star seems, at first dazzle, to shine brightest for her own sex. She inspires the doting mum, cheers the bored young housewife and jaded secretary, puts flesh and clothes on the daydreams of schoolgirls. As one magazine cover had it, she is 'spreading happiness wherever she goes'.

But, as she and her female devotees gaze into the enchanted mirror that throws back the Princess as the perfect model of contemporary femininity, they must take note of another, shadowy figure there: the Prince over her shoulder, without whom none of this would have been possible. And, crowded behind him, her loyal private army of photographers who would, can, and do walk through fire, mud, rain and near-avalanche to be close to her, and make perpetual vicarious lensman's love to her. Without *them* none of this would have been possible. Prince and paparazzi between them endorse and exalt Diana as the ultimate epitome of What Men Currently Want.

What do they see in her? What special chemistry makes her The One? There is, of course, the obvious and simple answer: she is young and beautiful; she appeared at a time when morale was low and the Royal Family's torch was fading. But that does not alone explain her deeper, universal appeal. '*Everybody* fancies her,' protested royal reporter James Whitaker, when his wife accused him of becoming besotted with his target. Nigel Dempster was more detached: 'To men she is a sex symbol; to women she is a clothes symbol.' Which amounts, more or less, to the same thing.

Diana's wardrobe has in a sense been one long and varied mating display – to the Prince in particular and to British manhood in *other papers/books say "wonderful"*

general. She dresses and is dressed to be the perfect adjunct, Mrs Right of their dreams. 'You look beautiful,' the lip-readers saw Charles tell his bride when she arrived at the altar on the wedding day. 'Beautiful for you,' came the reply, pat as one of her step-grandmother's best heroines, but touching in its simplicity all the same.

At the outset, then, she was the innocent, the virgin, the old-fashioned sweetheart, wooed and wed (with benefit of press attendance) according to the best, most romantic book. She was thus a sexual prize, a social asset and object of competition, almost at times a quarry to be chased. And at times, fittingly, she ran. She ran from the photographers, sometimes as if enjoying the heady fun of suddenly being the centre of pursuit and attention, sometimes in panic, as when she deserted her then famous Mini Metro car in the middle of the London traffic and fled into the crowd in hysterics, leaving the shame-faced hacks to slink back to her flat and push notes of love and apology through the letter-box. Sometimes she even seemed to be running from the very situation she most longed to achieve. A (male) guest at the pre-Wedding ball at Buckingham Palace recalls her tall, thin, wide-eyed figure running like a startled wild creature along the balcony of the ballroom and away from the throng. 'She looked frightened and lost and so very young,' he said. And later as a reputedly bored and lonely new wife at Highgrove she is said to have run out of the house in her dressing gown, jumped into a car and roared off into the night. 'I just had to get out for a bit,' she apologized to a frantic security man later.

Innocent, helpless, lost. She was also refreshing, a born-again good girl, ready to take on her assigned role. 'It's what I want,' she said simply. And she wore her pearls, a symbol of purity, in a choker, the symbol of domination. After flying free she was bagged and transformed into a caged bird who, after momentary signs of pining and fading away, and a little fluttering against the bars, settled on her perch and grew ever more beautiful, ever more powerful and desirable, the untouched and untouchable. Her hair, once mousy, became blonder, blond being the colour of fun, happy sexuality, but also the colour of gold and slavery. Ever since the

Roman women started dyeing their dark hair blond in emulation of their German slave girls, Western gentlemen have preferred it. Our Princess also grew her hair from its chunky girlish crop into a thick, luxuriant tangle.

In so doing she may have been making an unconscious sexual announcement: 'I'm grown up now, I know how to look, how to dazzle you all. I no longer need to be ordered about. I know my power.' The new assertive flamboyance did not please one of her earliest courtiers, a man who claimed with some justification to have done most to create Diana's image. Her hairdresser Kevin Shanley, who had been keeping the famous fringe in shape and check since before the engagement, and who had been one of her first confidants about the impending announcement, was horrified when she insisted on growing her hair and talked of putting it up. Her husband, she explained, to counter this male objection, would like to see it up. But there was a feeling that this male authority was being invoked only because it suited the Princess's own whim. She had her way, as we have seen, and the rejected Svengali had to console himself by selling his 'salon secrets' to a Sunday newspaper in which he re-counted his clashes with the Princess, culminating in his sending his partner to do Diana's hair for the formal pictures of the newborn Prince Harry. It is from these pictures that the 'Dynasty Di' nick-name dates: 'It wasn't her . . . it was someone else, glossy, plastic and very, very American. It was as though she had stepped off the set of a TV soap opera or the production line at the Sindy Doll factory,' wrote Shanley. Growing up is hard to do, so is growing out.

Diana tried a number of different styles after this, but she has never gone back completely to her little girl look. 'La Princesse Sexy' (a 1984 cover-line from Paris Match) has held her own and continues to appeal to men by looking marvellous and saying little. She even makes a point of mocking her own intellectual weightlessness with a running joke about what lies under the much disputed locks:

Royal hatter: 'Oh, ma'am, what a big head you've got.'
Princess: 'Don't worry, there isn't anything in it.'

Lord Snowdon's formal portrait of Princess and baby, from which a new hairstyle and the nickname Dynasty Di date.

'She is the most perfect of today's princesses,' said an Italian journalist enthusiastically. 'Beautiful, silent, smiling, wonderfully still.' The same writer felt sorry, however, that such a young woman should only be asked her opinion about clothes and children. A man might have expressed the admiration without the sympathy. For, in her stillness and beauty and limited intellectual range Diana appears as the affluent society's perfect wife. A creature to desire, chase, catch and tame, then to shelter and impregnate, and cover with the protective umbrella of home, status and all good things that a man on the right track in a consumerist world can provide.

Although Diana 'works' very hard and likes to be described as a 'working mum', her 'work' is mainly representational, and she appears to advertise, in effect, the old middle-class housewife stereotype of the Fifties, revived and rejuvenated and elevated: a captive, indulged woman who dominates by being dominated. In this uncomfortable paradox lies the power of the whole dilemma-ridden deal struck between men and women since the invention of the vacuum cleaner and the washing machine, and the dissolution of the servant classes.

The ethos which spawned all the little woman sitcom TV series of the Fifties, from *I Love Lucy* to *I Married Joan*, required a woman to give up her worldly freedoms and independent mind, while man handed over his social identity and his washing for her to manage instead. In this bargain, a wife becomes a husband's justification and his excuse; she is also his advertisement, and a vital part of his credentials. She sets his tone, and may determine everything from his friends to his diet and the colour of his pyjamas. He has power; she has control. He may own the family house; she is in charge of it. He may earn the money; she will decide how to spend it. The lady gives permissions, grants favours, maintains morality, and the old courtly tradition lives on.

As a result a man may possess but feel dispossessed, somehow excluded from the centre of his own life. The writer and broadcaster Anna Ford in her documentary book on men noted that, when men wanted to weep, they often retired to the greenhouse or potting shed to do it, because they had no privacy in their own houses nor permission to show emotion in public. The trap is obvious but hard to get out of: if you take on dependants, that is what they are, and forever after you will have to be dependable.

Society is, of course, arranged to give men some respite from all this. They have many diversions and recreations, which may be vigorous and 'manly', sporting ones, or time- and body-wasting inactivities like propping up the bar, or furtive and off-limits distractions like love affairs and visits to the strip-club. The time is gone when a double life could be conducted openly.

In Royal terms, Edward VII was the last monarch to do so blatantly. He maintained an exemplary marriage to a beautiful woman; he also indulged in a colourful and hedonistic extra-marital life. But he was already an anachronism, and, two world wars and half a century later, Queen Elizabeth and Prince Philip presented the model of the perfect modern nuclear family . . . suburban in style if palatial in substance and structure, a way of life everyone could recognize, relate to and even emulate on a different scale. The Queen's reign has demonstrated that, whatever the monarchy lacks in executive power, it makes up for in social and moral influence. The emergence of Diana added the pzazz and glamour of show business and fairy tales.

She is the first convincing princess of the video age, symbolizing, as we have seen, golden girlhood, romantic sexuality – just as Brigitte Bardot stood for more torrid, lustful, liberated sex in *her* generation. But, because Diana also represents the return of the wifely ideal, built on powerful passivity and dependence, the sex princess is much more powerful than the sex kitten or the delectable piece of fluff.

She offers, for a start, opportunities not just for fantasies and photography, but for ritual displays of gallantry and protectiveness. The early women's movement was much preoccupied with men in their brutish, violent manifestations: rapists, bullies, batterers and plain old male chauvinist pigs overshadowed the Galahads and gallants. Having their apparently good and gentle side rejected was the single most hurtful thing men suffered from feminism. Being called MCPs was fine; being told their protective and courteous instincts were unwanted was the equivalent of telling women their maternal feelings were not genuine, or no longer required.

But who or what does a woman need protecting against? First and foremost other men – rivals, marauders and monsters alike. So obviously the ultra-feminine woman in high heels and cinched waist and flimsy dress, being more attractive and more hampered, is more in need of guarding than the commando-type in flying suit and sneakers.

Prince Charles is unlikely to clamp his princess into a chastity belt, but she has a cordon around her (of hefty security men and delicate clothes) which many older husbands of beautiful young wives might envy. The 'sexier' her image becomes, the more this vigilance and protection seems necessary. Diana explained that the silver dress with a cut-away back was not always suitable because 'people, when they guide you, sometimes do not know where to put their hands.' In Italy, in Spring 1985, there was a rumour among the press corps that a special anti bottom-pinching unit of the *carabinieri* had been recruited to protect the princessly backside. In the event, perhaps to make the point, the only person who pinched her bottom was Charles himself, in full view of the cameras.

Back home, when it was decided that she needed a female addition to the force of police 'minders' protecting her from rather graver threats, there was some problem finding a volunteer from among the dozen or so London policewomen entitled to carry a gun. They were not, it seems, keen on the notion of dressing up to follow the Princess to the bathroom. 'I don't want to be a Sloane with a shooter,' said one drily.

Not all protectiveness is simple jealousy or bodyguarding. There is a deep-seated, conditioned need in most men to shelter, feed and fight for a family: something worth working for, dying for, going to war for. Take away the 'minder' role and men have little left to them. Philandering and helping with the nappies and washing up aren't enough. Small wonder they are more upset at the rejection of the old courtesies and door-opening than they are about the evils of rape and wife-battering. Diana brought hand-kissing back into its own.

Two royal images of modern manhood: Andrew, the roaring bonehead, spraying the press with paint . . .

. . . and Charles, the nappy-changing, caring dad, who wants to stay home and 'go cootchy-coo' with the babies.

It was, however, ironic that, just as the Princess appeared as the patron saint of the olde worlde, and the feminist peace movement was being labelled by many, from the British Minister of Defence downwards, as a minority KGB-backed conspiracy of dour, humourless lesbians, men were beginning to say and show that they had after all felt the effect of a decade of consciousness-raising and social revolution.

There were two extremes of reaction: the pro-feminist New Men, allegedly in touch with their finer feelings and longing to share more fully in the care of their children and domesticity generally, and the over-the-top ultra-macho Real Men. In between lay all shades of androgyny and greyness, but the basic polarization seemed to be between the idiot husband who, in the TV commercials, means well but can't really cope with domestic rituals such as operating a toaster, and the old leather-skinned cowboys who are still out on the range, seeking a home where the buffalo roam.

The Royal Family, on cue, offered us good examples of each. If Prince Charles is the caring, nappy-changing New Man who, as one observer said, 'wants to stay home and go cootchy-coo with the babies', worries about conservation, the arts and his role, and treats his wife like a piece of porcelain, then his brother Andrew is the roaring bonehead, whose red rather than blue blood seems to pulse ever louder to remind us that the spirit of the stone age, never mind the age of chivalry, is not dead.

It was, however, the wimp and not the cowboy, the new rather than the trad man who married the Princess to make up the happy family model which the spirit and government of the time demanded.

7

*The rest of the book is not
worth reading – just claptrap –
except to pick out the bit re
Diana*

The Icon and the Living Dolls

The equation of the words 'pretty girl' with the word 'princess' is a familiar and coy cliché. 'My little princess' is a common enough term of endearment from doting father – or mother – to a small daughter. Toys and clothes have 'princess' in their labels and trademarks; there is a pre-teen girls' comic called *Princess*. Even such sophisticates as Robert Lacey, the writer, and Michael Rand, the designer, could not resist dedicating their book *Princess* to their daughters (Selina and Scarlett), dubbing them fondly 'our princesses'. It can be double edged: 'Jewish princess' and 'American princess' are common tags for spoilt, over-protected daughters of the rich.

'My father always called me "princess" when he was being affectionate and sometimes when he was teasing me for being uppish,' recalls a young woman of the same age as the real Princess of Wales. 'I liked it when I was little, because I knew that it meant he thought I looked pretty, that he was proud of me and loved me more than he loved my mother, who was the authoritarian one in our household. Later, I started to resent it and get embarrassed. He was much too protective and possessive. I think it was because I was the only girl and he didn't really want me to grow up.'

Even women who remember childhood with too little, rather than too much love, can recall turning to the princess myth for comfort. One, whose parents rejected her to the point of denying that she was their child ('My mother said she'd been given the wrong baby in the hospital: my father said she'd been unfaithful. I was a changeling'), read herself into fairy tales: 'I was always the princess. I felt frozen, asleep, as if life had not yet become real for me. I was waiting for the prince to come and bring me out of the sleeping life into the real life . . .'

To think of herself as a princess is an obvious form of escapism for the lonely or insecure little girl. She can place herself centre-stage, and become powerfully passive, someone for and to whom things are done, an object of love, someone to be placated and indulged. Helena Bonham-Carter, playing Lady Jane Grey in the recent film of that name, described her first experience of being a leading lady as 'being like royalty. People are at my beck and call and I only have to hint that I am craving for a Marmite sandwich and I get six in three minutes . . . it's as if I am wearing a label round my neck saying Handle With Care – nobody wants to be responsible for upsetting me.'

For, if you upset the princess, you upset the applecart. In the stories such trivial pampering does not spoil or suffocate the lady (although it may bore her and send her off in search of swineherds); in real life things may be more difficult and contradictory. How does anyone reconcile vulnerability and fragility with energy, intelligence, the will to action? The dilemma, some would argue, is inherent in being female in the first place: the princess myth, with all its implications of power and dependence, is part of a necessary, or at least inevitable, feminine conditioning in a structured, 'civilized' patriarchy. It endorses a particular form of family hierarchy, makes women a focus and advertisement for affluence; but it also contributes to what the American writer Colette Dowling called 'the Cinderella complex': 'a network of largely repressed attitudes and fears that keep women in a kind of half light, retreating from the full use of their minds and creativity. Like Cinderella, women today are still waiting for something external to transform their lives.'

Ms Dowling published her polemic in 1981. She was one of those who began to see and say that political and economic egalitarianism (which had not been achieved anyway) were not enough: something far deeper and more ingrained was going to have to shift before

Is the princess myth, with all its implications of power and dependence, part of an inevitable feminine conditioning, in a structured, 'civilized' patriarchy?

change would be possible. Like many others she was forced to the conclusion that this could only come from *within* women themselves. An old, lonely truth.

But there are also external factors working against notions of self-responsibility and equality for women; unemployment, inflation, fear of war, a rising tide of reaction, with its reassertion of old values which place women firmly in the home – or in a glass case, or on the shelf, or in whatever confinement suits the circumstance. All the vigorous feminist debate has, it appears, done little to change basic cultural ideas about women. In some ways it has reinforced them. Indeed 'feminist' has become a new stereotype, an image to add to the existing range. It is, if you like, at one end of the seesaw, with 'princess' at the other, and mother, housewife, superwoman, sex object, etc., somewhere in between. And, like all stereotypes, it is a kind of trap, conferring an instant two-dimensional quality on the person so dubbed. In the case of 'feminist' it is a two-dimensional ugliness, humourlessness and general grimness that make the word increasingly difficult to use. Perhaps that has always been the case: Rebecca West once wrote that she didn't know what the word meant, but that people used it of her every time she tried to speak as if she was neither a doormat nor a whore. Certainly, since the days of the suffragettes, women who step out of the doll's house, or sweat shop or even just out of domestic line, and too vocally try to change ideas about what women ought to be, how they ought to speak, look, or behave, have been seen as, at best, sillies and, at worst, dangerous subversives.

Sometimes they have been either or both: there have indeed been many active feminist Marxists, socialists and anarchists. But, in general, scare-mongering about feminism's political affiliations or intentions is usually a way of dodging the real issue that it raises. It is the attempt to move the icon of femininity away from its assigned place above the family hearth that causes the real trouble. When it *has* been shifted it has had to be moved back again, sharpish, by fair means or foul. The Second World War required British and American women to 'liberate' themselves, put work outside the home first. The post-war period required a quick reversal of this.

The ultra-feminine style of the Fifties was one of the most contrived and artificial – that is dependent on every artifice from lipstick to corsetry and hair bleach – since the days of crinolines, whalebones and ringlets. Women had dressed functionally, to match their functions, during the Second World War. If they were not actually in uniform, then they were in unfussy, tailored clothes. There was not, in any case, any fabric to waste or flaunt, and it would have seemed unpatriotic to indulge in fripperies when there was a war on.

Predictably, when peace came, the coin flipped. Dior's famous New Look, with its long, rustling skirts and tiny waist, was the reassertion of a trend held over from the Thirties, and now became the frivolous, luxurious start of the era which saw the revival of the 'little woman' and the big-busted, baby-voiced Marilyn Monroe emerge as the chief sex symbol and fantasy figure. Sugar – the character played by Monroe in *Some Like It Hot* – was back on the menu. And, for a time, it seemed that rationality went out the window with the ration books.

The young of the Fifties rocked and jived to Elvis and Buddy Holly in starched petticoats and mini-crinnies, their nipped-in waists and cone-shaped breasts projecting a cardboard cut-out femininity, while their mothers enjoyed the fruits of victory by cooking them, back in their own kitchens. For the affluent, and especially in America, it was the age of gadgetry and housewifery, and ever-improving washing powder. It was also the time of that exquisite and dangerous accoutrement, the stiletto heel, and the beginning of the age of the tranquillizer. Then in 1963, Betty Friedan published her famous treatise *The Feminine Mystique*, identifying pampered domestic loneliness as the cause of the 'illness without a name'. With this she helped, it is said, to ignite the torch of the women's liberation movement.

The irony is that the tough and resilient, and, to some, threatening, image of feminism grew cheek-by-jowl with one of extreme, vapid passivity. The swinging Sixties in Britain projected girls and young women as usable, available, exploitable creatures who could be taken almost at will without compassion, guilt or fear of post-coital complaint. They were passive, provocative, asking for it. It

(*Left*) The Fifties saw the revival of the little woman, with the big-busted, baby-voiced Marilyn Monroe as the chief sex symbol and fantasy figure.

(*Below*) In the Sixties, girls were passive and provocative. Twiggy, with her featureless body and beautiful, sad, Coppelia's face seemed to starve in the sight of plenty.

was no longer either chic or contraceptively necessary for a girl to be chaste. Sex was a free for all: the popular face of the decade was wide-eyed and vacuous; the body child-like and unfecund, hungry for male imprint for its own sake. The photographer became, not a flirt nor a courtier as previously, but a sexual aggressor, almost a rapist. The domestic icon was at risk far more from the gravure images of the time than it was from the rather drab and anonymous if assertive face of feminism. Models were, even more than actresses, the acme of glamorous womanhood. Anything went, especially virginity. The mini-skirt and flat chests and long necks and legs gave these living dolls a manipulable, puppet-like quality.

Jean Shrimpton ('The Shrimp'), Penelope Tree (aptly named) and, most of all, Twiggy (aptly nicknamed) with her featureless body and sad, beautiful Coppelia's face, seemed to starve in the sight of plenty. Gone were the grandes dames and ballerinas and mannequins who had married millionaires, or looked as if they might; and gone too were the sex kittens à la Bardot who pouted and lured and promised without threatening.

Instead, there was the curious blend of innocence and ignorance which was defiled but took no responsibility for its defilement. There was the little-girl-lost of the decade, 'convent educated' Marianne Faithfull perched on a stool singing *As Tears Go By* too sweetly for words, but who offered us also the sexual image of the decade – Mick Jagger eating Mars bars out of her vagina. Indeed mouths and vaginas seemed for a time interchangeable and their owners at times seemed too stoned or too dumb to know which was which.

In *Girls on Film* (Proteus, 1983), Julie Burchill noted the contradiction:

It seems impossible that the Sixties was the time of feminist breakthrough in America when one compares the celluloid evidence with that of the Thirties. See Harlow and West wise-cracking their way through life; see Garbo and Dietrich use the world as their stage. In the Sixties, gape disbelievingly at the almost impossibly underdeveloped characters that, say, Katherine Ross is called upon to sleepwalk through in *Butch Cassidy and the Sundance Kid* and *The Graduate* . . . women who wait and are grateful.

The vapid 'heroines' noted by Burchill are still with us, although sometimes they find a despairing voice. Witness the young wife in the Wim Wenders/Sam Sheppard film *Paris, Texas*: only finally, from inside a glass box where she is paid to act out situation-and-role-fantasies for men, is she able to talk to her husband, who sits like a peepshow client on the outside, seeing but unseen, listening to her for the first time.

When George Lucas was devising *Star Wars*, he knew he had to create a princess character: 'somebody the guys can rescue'. In the first synopsis they were to be rewarded by the princess on her home planet, where she reveals her true 'goddess-like self'. 'Then we made her a teenager,' said Lucas. Her age later dropped to eleven, but rose again to sixteen for the version on which the project was sold. By this time she 'has the mind-control powers of a witch, and is captured and tortured by the villains'. But whatever changes and revisions her character underwent, 'We always kept her a princess,' Lucas told his biographer, Dale Pollock. 'It just does not work if she isn't a princess.'

In both history and fairy tales, princesses have been little more than pawns in a game, symbols of power or perfect, inaccessible sexuality, or both. They may have been used to cement an alliance or to continue a dynasty. They talk in platitudes if they talk at all. Not until the appearance of Diana, Princess of Wales, had one been used as a living role model for the masses.

It is part of Diana's success that she seems closer to the High Street than any temple of haute couture. Simply by slimming, and dressing beautifully and conventionally, and by having two children and a rich husband, she represents the reactionary dreams of her generation.

Where has this new conservatism sprung from? What happened to the dreams of equality, liberation, independent achievement? Tina Brown, writing in *Tatler*, unofficial gazette of London's café society, in 1981 described Lady Diana Spencer, as she was then, as 'one of a generation of born-again good girls who choose to play it safe. The career girls, the rebels, the bolters, the experimenters are now among the older generation . . . she knows what she has missed and doesn't care.'

Brown was writing about the English upper-crust, about Sloane Rangers and ravers; but what she notes serves as a reminder to those who point to feminism as a misleader and disappointer of women. What disappointed far more than ideology were notions that sexual liberation was truly possible for young women, that the old morality was defunct, that the Pill made for freedom and the new technology meant babies could be timed and made to order. 'Too many girls were,' as Katharine Whitehorn, the London *Observer*'s columnist, puts it, 'conned into a *male* idea of liberation' and laid themselves wide open to exploitation as a result. A woman's right to choose too often meant a man's right to abuse.

The new generation may not be so easily duped, but they may be forgiven for feeling a little confused by a culture at odds with social reality in a different way. While the government approves and actively fosters pro-family policies and people still talk about the 'family' as if the nuclear foursome needed no more than a new wardrobe before being put back on display, while romantic novelists continue to weave dreams of passionate courtship and nuptial bliss, government statistics present a picture of increasing divorce and single parenthood, of a declining birth and marriage rate.

The new propaganda runs something on the lines that 'It's all right, girls, you can forget all that stupid stuff about feminism and being free. The old way is the best and safest after all.' *Woman's Own*, a mass circulation weekly, can put Diana, holding toddler William, on the cover with the strapline 'Guess who's made mother-hood OK again?' Claire Rayner, a popular British agony aunt who is supposed to be more closely in touch with women's problems than most, wrote in that issue that women, thanks to feminist activity and thinking, began to be *ashamed* of their deeper feelings: 'They learned to pretend to despise those few of their sisters who shrugged off the political exhortations to be Modern Women and went serene-ly ahead doing what they wanted to do, which was have babies and enjoy them. The New Women actually did throw the babies out with the bath water.'

Rayner goes on to assess Diana's family style as being at least as influential as her clothes – 'Young marriage and early motherhood

are not just permitted again – they have become a perfectly reason-
able choice for the intelligent, educated young woman to make' –
and curiously to assert that this has been achieved by Diana 'almost
singlehanded'! 'She is in every sense of the word what the modern
mother is all about,' continues Rayner. 'Which means she has
turned the tide that has washed over women these past twenty-five
years and made them ashamed of their own needs. By being what
she is, young and in love with life in all its aspects and proud of her
parenthood, she has given women back to themselves.'

A heavy responsibility to lay at the door of a twenty-three-year-
old, and one which bears small relevance to the facts. Rayner attributes far more potency to 'feminist-based ideas' than they ever had
in practice. True, twentieth-century feminism preaches a gospel of
equality and self-responsibility, tending to over-emphasize work
outside the home as salvation, instead of trying to raise the status of
existence *inside* it. But that is perhaps something not even five
Princesses of Wales could do. A far more influential gospel was the
commercial one: if you had your own job and money, you could buy
your own clothes, car, house, have your own lovers and orgasms and
stay young forever. The snag was, you had to *work* for it. Part of the
appeal of the princess myth to the young is that she has it all without
having to dirty her hands. She promotes the notion of passivity, of
woman as status symbol who works at being nothing more than
herself.

This is quite simply a revival of the old stereotype of the hothouse
housewife, the bird in a gilded cage. It is, in a more glamorous guise,
the very stereotype that the whole feminist movement rose up to
destroy. Now, in times of unemployment, the safety of a home paid
for by the sweat of another's brow seems, once more, far to over-ride
any threat of boredom or unfulfilment. The trick is to marry, if not
the prince, at least a man rich enough to keep you in the manner of
your fantasy.

Rayner was wrong, of course, to suggest sweepingly that women
spent the Sixties and Seventies bathing in a tide of shame, pretend-
ing they didn't want children and didn't need men. If they weren't
sitting around longing to be discovered as a model or an actress, they

tended (and this Diana's heiresses can see quite clearly) to wear
themselves out trying to balance two roles – domestic and bread-
winning. Playing Superwoman was an exhausting business and,
perhaps, half the health and fitness obsession of the Seventies and
Eighties is a spin-off from those stresses. But following the feminist
example looked like a kind of emotional and social suicide to the
majority. Feminism, for all the force and influence of its ideas,
provided probably the least appealing stereotype; it *seemed* to require women to turn their back on all the good and easy things of
life, including, and especially, men.

Feminism, curiously, became in retrospect the whipping post for
everything that went wrong with the sexual revolution. Liberation
was confused with libertarianism and libertinism; sexual responsibility and freedom of choice was to blame for promiscuity.

Having begun in kitchens and women's groups and universities
and refuges for battered wives, feminism had led, by the year of the
Royal Wedding, not to some nirvana of equality or manlessness, but
to the uncomfortable bivouacs outside the wire fences of the US
military base at Greenham Common in Berkshire, one of England's
home counties deep in the heartland of conservatism. England's
green and pleasant land, the Greenham women insisted on reminding people uncomfortably, was planted with more than apple trees
and barley. These days dark, satanic missiles were polluting Jeru-
salem.

The changes and stages of the Greenham women's image is a
fascinating reflection of what happens when society's basic and
acceptable female stereotype is threatened too seriously. When the
first thirty women set out from Wales in 1981, they were 'mothers
and housewives' campaigning for peace. It was only a matter of
weeks before they became 'feminists' then 'hard-line feminists',
then 'lesbians'. Later still they were grotesques, harridans, KGB-
funded dupes or agents, a disgrace to their gender. The police called
them 'smellies' and were forbidden eye-contact with them, as were

The development of the Greenham Woman's image is a reflection of what
happens when society's basic and acceptable female stereotype is threatened.

US personnel. Paul Johnson, right-wing commentator, called them 'woolly hats on woolly minds'. The government was moved to appoint a full-time minister, a blond beast whose nickname was 'Tarzan', to deal with the anti-nuclear women problem.

Visiting Greenham during this time it was easy to see how the 'unsavoury' image could be used against them. The camp looked rather like a makeshift community constructed by the survivors of a nuclear attack. The women lived in tents or benders, igloo-like constructions of plastic sheeting and branches. They spent the day in the open, sitting round a campfire on old boxes and tyres and armchairs, drinking eternal cups of tea, discussing tactics and rotas and excursions and waiting for news, just like any siege army. They were tired, grubby, living frugally, and off occasional luxuries like chocolate biscuits brought in by well-wishers. And yet, as Martha Gellhorn, war correspondent and former Mrs Hemingway to boot, noted, it was the men – the police on guard, and the paratroopers bobbing about on armoured cars, exercising and building observation towers inside the wire – who seemed trapped.

The women certainly looked a raggle-taggle lot. It would have been easy to come away and declare them, by sight alone, to be a rout of extreme feminists bent on disrupting the country's defence system and plotting to invite the Russians to share their firesides. And indeed there *were* committed feminists and lesbians there. There were also intellectuals, librarians, teachers and grandmothers. There was chewed-off short hair, but there were also long silky braids, Queen Elizabeth II perms, expensive bobs and the North London worthy tousles, all put together round the campfires. It was cold, and certainly many of their clothes and hats did, indeed, seem to be made of wool. In their anoraks and mufflers and wellies, they might have been an all-female football crowd; the kind of mix you might find in any city bus queue in winter. The younger women seemed more urban than the older. The first person to greet me on arrival was a hearty soul in a yellow polo-neck jumper, curly, short hair and apple-red cheeks. She was a shopkeeper from Essex, whose three sons were paying for her vigil at Greenham and kept her supplied with food and good cheer. There was a chic lady in leather boots and a well-cut hacking jacket who hailed from Sheffield; at one point a sturdy local farmer's wife stumped in to ask if they needed any more milk and eggs.

There were freaks too. A woman who called herself 'Black' and painted herself silver sat in the bender nearest the main gate. 'I am a black witch,' she announced solemnly to explain her name. The hand of spade cards ceremoniously displayed among candles, dolls and other superstitious nick-nacks were of ill omen, she said, but only for policemen.

Outside, the women were collecting candles and mirrors for which they planned a symbolic use at the next big demonstration. The idea had come from a woman who had brought a large mirror to the camp – quite rare. 'We don't care what we look like; it's not the place for vanity,' someone explained. Suddenly, one day, the mirror owner had walked up to the fence with her glass and held it up facing the soldiers inside, so that they could see themselves, not her, when they looked through the wire – which was of course also reflected.

The reaction had been educational, the women thought. Some of the men had clowned about and made faces and others looked away unnerved or irritated. But the longer she stood there, the more the foolery and discomfiture turned to hostility, abuse and something, the women claimed, that looked like fear. Certainly, looking in a mirror is a difficult thing to do, unless you have written your script first. If you are playing soldiers, what you want to see is the target, the enemy, not yourself. There was a plan to ring the whole base with women holding mirrors; it didn't work very well, but the idea was an intriguing one.

I have dwelt on Greenham because of its impact, and because it is the most controversial piece of feminist activism since suffragism. But also because the protest has been used mercilessly by the media, not to discredit the anti-cruise missile cause, but to discredit the *image* of feminism in general.

I have quoted Rayner at length because hers was one of the most direct statements of the new reactionary credo in a popular medium. Her article, published while the Greenham protest was at its height, was followed on the very next page by Douglas Keay, veteran royal commentator and show-biz interviewer, who struggled to present the Princess as a 'working mum', attempting to show how well she combines her 'job' with motherhood, a line which the Palace happily promotes too.

'She loves her work and even when she has an off day she knows well enough how to smile and keep smiling. It's called performing a royal duty. To many women her age it would often seem a hard slog – with compensations admittedly.' Keay tells us how reluctant the Princess is to leave her babies when she is working, but how she is cheered by the way people ask her about them everywhere she goes. Having to leave your babies in the line of duty is sad but O K; to abandon them in the line of political or pacifist activism is not.

On a wittier, more ironic level in the *Mail on Sunday* magazine *You*, Rachel Billington (novelist daughter of Lord Longford) considered the new, proud, post-feminist female partner: 'Something happened to the wife around about 1970. She went into a black hole, the one with the oven in it perhaps. At any rate she became invisible. She was in hiding while her angry sister the Feminist took centre stage.' Billington explains how 'feminist-induced guilt took the joy out of her crisp summer curtains, her children's shiny shoes, her husband's knife-edged creases. Now she can relax a little . . . it's such a relief to be allowed to be a wife again.' Relief has come, of course, from the Princess of Wales, whose smiling picture complete with adoring husband dominates the article (although Ann Parkinson, wife of the disgraced ex-Chairman of the Tory Party, and Mrs Lech Walesa are among the others who got gold stars).

At the end of it all, Billington comes clean and says she personally believed in something called the 'Feminist-Wife'. 'Strong, loyal, an ever-ready porous rock for the cares and problems of her husband and children. She is also independent, ambitious, brave and in the end answerable to herself.'

It would be nice to believe that this paragon was a commonplace, not a rare bird: it's hard not to see that the prevailing cultural wind is blowing against her, as it did last time around:

Nothing seemed to have worked out as it had been expected. The women of the Thirties began to react against the triumphant feminism of the Twenties. Girls, instead of persisting in wishing for a career, began again to say that they hoped to marry. The reasons for this were twofold. First the shortage of jobs for men, secondly the prizes of emancipation turned out not to be so glamorous as they had seemed in prospect.

Quentin Crewe in *The Frontiers of Privilege* (Collins, 1961), a retrospective book about *Queen* magazine, goes on to quote a Thirties' contributor:

This glorious freedom, how much of it did we really need? What have we gained in addition? The privilege of doing men's chores and our own as well but without being thanked for it this time.

Writing nearly fifty years on, Jacqueline Sarsby in *Romantic Love and Society* (Penguin, 1983) conducted a survey of adolescent attitudes to expectations of love and found that girls hold apparently old-fashioned views of love and marriage, and are in a sense untouched by the feminist movement because they grasp a deep social truth.

Their marriage is going to determine their status and lifestyle, and all their energies have to be channelled into the competitive search for the best partner they can attract . . . In the midst of the myth of equality, the romantic myth hides only an unwelcome reality.

And here is one touchstone to the 'overwhelming' appeal of the Princess of Wales. Not at all by her own seeking, and perhaps not even to her knowledge, she has become the symbol of the perfect working of romance and reality.

8

Of Wise and Foolish Virgins

Romance of the kind the story of Diana and Charles is said to represent is always being revived, rather as if it had somehow died, or was sleeping like Snow White herself. In fact, although it may slip from the front line of fashion and be scorned by 'serious' thinkers, romance never dies out of 'popular' taste and imagination. A romantic revival usually means merely the reassertion of a kind of reactionary chic.

Sophisticates may argue a little about the precise dating of the most recent exhumation, which seemed to react against the cynicism, street wisdom and social conscience of the Sixties and Seventies. Was it that month in 1978 when *Vogue* put 'Love' back on the cover, filled its glossy pages with misty pictures of lingerie, a feature on the gardens of Buckingham Palace and a fairy story, *Beauty and the Beast* retold by Angela Carter? Or was it five years earlier, when Kenzo ordered us back into long skirts? Or much later, after the Princess and the Falklands campaign, not to mention movies such as *Chariots of Fire*, had, in their different ways, tugged at an ancient island pride?

Whatever your special susceptibility, 'romance' is a cloudy, veiling word, defensive rather than aggressive, a symptom of reaction rather than progress. As Roman Polanski lamented in January 1984 looking back to his Sixties heyday: 'A woman must feel very confident, not at all vulnerable, to wear a mini-skirt. Now women go out in an armour.'

Romance looks inwards and backwards. It is where we turn when realities prove too dull or painful or dangerous, problems too doggedly insoluble. By definition, romance indicates the beautiful unreal, a fantasy of the world as we wish it to be, rather than as it is.

It also rests more on feelings than facts. The great Romantic poets exercised their creativity on an *emotionally* perceived reality, in which love, or nature, conquered all, and unattainable beauty was worth striving for. They understood the implicit tragedy in their stance: 'We look before and after for what is not'; and in the pursuit of 'Joy whose hand is ever at his lips bidding adieu'. But still the doomed Keats could write that he was 'certain of nothing but the holiness of the heart's affections and the truth of imagination.' Generations of English schoolgirls have embraced his philosophy as their own, at their own level.

In the 1980s we are back to a hothouse romanticism, set in drawing rooms and penthouses and personal lives and, above all, in the scripts of glossy television soap operas. The 'new', or revived, romance centres once more around the oldest myth of all – that of lost innocence, a longing for the restoration of sweetness, light and purity, salvation after a time of dissolution and corruption. Youth is the cipher, female youth in particular: as in all English fiction, from Cordelia to Jane Eyre to Rebecca, innocent women are angels of redemption, or angels to be redeemed.

Technical virginity lost its mystique briefly with the advent of modern methods of contraception, better education for girls (especially about their own bodies) and the burgeoning of ideas of equality and sexual freedom. This demystification was laced into feminist thought and talk of the Sixties, but it was fostered by commerce. Many a greedy and exploitative eye focused beadily on all those brave new girls, earning their own, if meagre, livings, suddenly believing that the whole world was indeed their oyster and hoping, among other things, to be able to enjoy rather than endure, or simply bargain with, sex. Such enjoyment had hitherto been associated with depravity, folly, nymphomania and impure badness. Nice girls didn't, certainly not for the hell of it or for pleasure. Sex was something you 'saved' and 'gave' to your husband, who was also meant to be your true love and would 'free' you.

The new magazines of the liberated age, of which *Cosmopolitan* was the prototype and most successful example, preached something different – how to get a man, a job and a multiple orgasm as well. They promoted an idea that sexual prowess and attractiveness, not money, social position or romantic love, would best snare a man, or better still, many men. You had to buy a lot of make-up, clothes and deodorants to do it, but that was part of the fun.

Nevertheless, Jacqueline Sarsby, whose *Romantic Love and Society* also studied women's magazine fiction of the early 1970s in Britain, found that the stories reflected women's dependent status: they worked, yes, but men earned more and rose higher, which meant that marriage to one of them was still the goal:

What the fiction described was a love-worship, not of women by men as in the Middle Ages, but of men by women. There was the same anxiety about marriage as in the 19th century, but with every girl for herself, making her own way in the world working in a white collar job with no fortune but her face and figure, and no dowry but her dress sense.

Later surveys reflected a change in sexual morality – divorce and extra-marital sex had become acceptable in the story lines – but still a persistence of the essentially domestic role of women, and an ever growing stature of the romantic hero: 'England is suddenly teeming with tall, ruggedly handsome men emerging from sunray lamps . . . heroines tend to have bosses but no careers if they are not married, husbands but no careers if they are,' notes Sarsby.

Thus dependence and romance are intertwined, and a providing man is still the prize. If girls and young women look beyond their magazines at the heroines of *Dallas* and *Dynasty* they will see more of the same: well-manicured, pampered bitches who tear and spit and even kill to get and keep a man and his riches. If they read the even sicker Cinderella stories of Shirley Conran and Judith Krantz and Jackie Collins, they will find women as sexual victims, embroiled in incest, soft porn, and all manner of fear and loathing before, perhaps, winning through to a revenge which usually means getting their pretty hands on the loot.

There are, of course, those storytellers who never permit their heroines to escape from their innocence to be humiliated in the manner of the heroine of *Lace*. Recently they have been saying 'I told you so', in a loud and convincing manner. One such has a deliciously close link with the Princess of Wales herself. What irony that Diana's step-grandmother – that is the mother of her step-mother – should turn out to be that great high priestess of romance and virginity, Barbara Cartland.

Miss Cartland cannot be accused of cashing in on her royal proximity since she has scarcely changed her line or her plots since long before Lady Diana Spencer was born. She was spiritedly ped-dling chastity and old values when everyone else was on about multiple orgasms and *Fear of Flying*. There are more than three hundred Cartland novels, in all of which young, pure girl wins through to good, wise, passionate man, who sweeps her off her feet and into an unknowable maturity behind closed doors. Titles include *A Virgin in Mayfair*, *A Virgin in Paris*, *Love Holds the Cards*, *Cupid Rides Pillion*, *The Elusive Earl*, *Never Laugh at Love*, and so on.

The author herself, a lady of unquenchable energy and incor-rigible promotional talent, has a similar taste, fortissimo, in feathers and furs and pastel colours to the Queen Mother's – the sort of grande dame style that has now more or less vanished, except from the wardrobes of the classier sort of drag artistes. Miss Cartland believes in honey, vitamins and assorted patent potions, just as much as she believes in virginity.

But the latter was, she insists, the whole key to her success: 'That's what has swept the world.' Her step-grandchild might have been invented just to prove the point. Indeed, Miss Cartland, with perfect delicacy, has made it clear that she feels vindicated and delighted at Diana's advancement.

What a delightful change, she and others might say, from the sad, or at least taxing, tales of the Sixties and Seventies when strivers after elusive truth, such as Margaret Drabble, created heroines of a drab suffering and pretentious intelligence, and Jacky Gillot could write that romance was 'compromise in fancy dress'.

In the new decade, the journalist Bel Mooney has written sadly that the renewed appetite for easier romances, as provided by Cart-land and the myriad Mills and Boon authors, might perhaps be an escape from the divorce figures, just as medieval courtly love masked 'the squalor, brutality and horse-trading of marriage'. These 'escapist' stories are narrow and stunted, for all that they may be entertaining or titillating. They permit of no third dimension, no complexity, no adulthood. Innocence equals lack of responsibility. As a mirror on the world they are about as useful as a television commercial for washing powder or Oxo. But if they are simply a way to an hour or two's distraction from the hard grind, what harm?

Escapism may be a genuine wish to escape from current sexual mores, but because it was not always easy to contrive a convincingly modern plot with a heroine as pure as the driven snow, many Cartland romances, as well as those by Denise Robins, Catherine Cookson and others, are set in the past, thus adding the furbelows of costume to the heat of dangerous, 'forbidden' or repressed passion, and disguising its contemporary relevance.

None of the doyennes of romantic fiction, however, were named as favourite authors by schoolgirls I questioned, while one much newer recruit to the genre, Jilly Cooper, appeared over and over again. She has succeeded in producing a series of novels which have witty and utterly contemporary scripts. She uses a neat and clever formula: each book has the name of its heroine as the title – *Emily*, *Harriet*, *Octavia*, etc. – and each cover carries a misty, blonde picture of the author. The plots, up to a point, follow the well-worn romantic tradition: a young innocent, orphaned or misunderstood girl is caught up in a train of events – often of a pretty melodramatic nature – from which she is ultimately rescued by the hero. The difference between Cooper romance and, say, a Mills and Boon standard work is that the dialogue is racy and funny and punny. She is, to boot, clearly creating a collection of modern morality tales in which virtue, not just sexual purity, is rewarded, and not only promiscuity, but selfishness and cruelty, are punished.

The stories are sexy without being soft-porn explicit, and their success may owe something to the revulsion in Diana's generation of 'born-again good girls' against the image of themselves not only as sex objects but as sexual performers and competitors. Certainly contemporary girls of between seventeen and twenty do not, when interviewed, seem at all keen to spread their legs and show off their pudenda in *Penthouse* magazine, although undeniably some of their age group and younger are doing it. They may also take care to keep the most devoted of boyfriends at arm's length and concentrate on True Love as allied to the future and security, rather than to instant gratification. They show a distinct taste for being wooed and calling the tune at the same time. What's more, it is chic to be chaste, or at least to put 'sex' far down your list of priorities.

There are plenty of object lessons for these maidens in Jilly Cooper's novels. Her Octavia, for example, is a rich and spoiled and very beautiful girl who treats everyone badly, sleeps around and thinks she can have what she wants. Her profligate life means that when the chips are down, right down, and her even more dissolute brother needs money, the only place she can earn it for him is in the pornographer's studio. She is, however, rescued at the eleventh hour by a rugged ape-like Celt (Cooper's heroes all owe more to Mr Rochester than to the hunk in the Marlboro ads) who appears 'fierce as ten furies, terrible as hell' among all the creeps who are victimizing her. He bears her off, and, after being quite fierce with her, proceeds to melt the sexual ice. The photographer had been urging Octavia to 'open her legs wide'; being a Cooper heroine she was able to come up with a joke – 'any minute he was going to ask me to say Ah' – but nevertheless felt 'like she had toads crawling all over her'. Later she has to confess that she has been to bed with so many men she can hardly remember, but that she hated it with all of them. 'I can put up a good act but inside I freeze up.' This latter-day Snow White may not match Cartland's requirements but has a kind of virginity all the same.

In *Imogen*, another moral tale from the Cooper canon, the cover-line actually announces that 'the life of a jet set virgin was a hard one'. Imogen, it turns out, is a vicar's daughter from Yorkshire, 'entirely untouched by human hand, which makes a change' and tempts a lascivious tennis player to take a bet on her defloration. He loses, and Imogen scores over him and the self-absorbed glamour-puss models squabbling over their nail polish and each other's men, by rescuing a baby from drowning.

None of Jilly Cooper's girls are prigs or prudes: most of them are

Marriage à la Mode

What!? Belinda wants to get **married**!? **NO**!? My God, **WHO** to?

To...this **Alistair**...one of the **directors** she helps cook for...**well, I** don't call it **COOKING**...What they **EAT** in that directors' dining room! You wouldn't **BELIEVE**!

But, what's he like, this..? Oh...**28**-ish...enormous income....drives a **SAAB**...–SIGH–

Oh dear!

They plan to live in his **mews** flat to start with.....

But Belinda can still work at her **career**, Wendy....

CAREER! Huh! That's the **last** thing she says she wants!

What's she going to do with herself, then, for Godsake? She's not **pregnant**, is she?

No, if she was, we'd be more understanding.

Well, it's her **bed**..she's got to lie on it...

Bloody comfy **BED**...she's ordering it at **Harrods**!

And she wants a **huge, WHITE** wedding....

NO!

Yes...and she wants poor George to **GIVE** her away–**can you imagine**?–like a chattel

NO!

© Posy Simmonds 1985

Whipped cream...lime jelly... ..crushed ginger biscuits ..it's *SUPPOSED* to e *Cordon Bleu*....

But it's more *Cordon Bleu-ch-ch!*

But, this is very sudden...

No...they've been carrying on some time....

So it seems

h, she'll keep herself ery *BUSY*...going to the airdresser...arranging affodils.....making rême brûlée...

All those *A levels* she's got.... The *WASTE!!*

It's *so irresponsible!* What's she going to do when the marriage *folds*? How's she going to support herself *then*?

She doesn't *THINK!*

Vow could Belinda *to* this to you!?...... ..After *ALL* you've...

I know!

We had such hopes for her... :SIGH: *Where* did we go wrong...?

I dunno *what* the neighbours'll say.....

Still, what can you do?...we'll stand by her...she *is* our daughter, after all...

I think I lay the blame at the feet of *Princess* Diana ..she set the young a terrible example just rather nice and silly, as Diana Spencer might have been, and in the mould of those who used to appear in fictionalized form as denizens of Enid Blyton's Malory Towers or Elinor M. Brent-Dyer's Chalet School.

This sort of romance, whether in Cartland or Cooper mode, is a peculiarly British addiction. As Veronica Horwell pointed out in the *Sunday Times*, it was the British who were responsible for the development of the novel, for *Pamela* and *Jane Eyre*, 'those romances and fantasies from which the modern product had developed. We had invented the Gothick tale with its toshy emotions and exotic locations and the circulating library with which it reached its clientele.' The managing director of Mills and Boon itself (which sells some 20 million books a year in Britain and abroad) declared that their customers were buying not just entertainment or distraction, but 'Reassurance and control. Control, that is, of chaos.' Control, perhaps, also of women's sexuality, although here the balance may have shifted a little: 'Heroines are as liberated as they choose to be, and heroes can no longer depend on the assumption that they are Prince Charming.' Happy endings, however, are still *de rigueur*.

Likewise the Diana myth has been sold to, and bought by, women. Women's magazines have provided the soapiest, most lavish coverage of her existence; Bob Houston knows that the readership of *Royalty* is 99.9 per cent female. Certainly, the world over which Diana will one day help to reign, but which for now she regards warily from under her golden hair and dramatic hats, *is* one of chaos and unpalatable and ever terrifying truths. Indeed some of the truths are so terrifying that anyone who draws too much attention to them is attacked with some of the hate and fear that might be better addressed to the problem. As the women of Greenham have found out, the bearer of bad news tends to get the punishment for it.

This is not to fall into the trap of saying 'fairy tales bad, feminist pacifist-activism good'. It is indeed possible to blame the women's movement as much as anyone else for the current 'romantic revival'.

Diana, Princess of Wales, combines the glamour of a movie star
with the power of the madonna – sexual yet untouchable.

Because, as Joan Didion has pointed out, so much of the movement became mired in trivia and indeed evasion of proper adult sexual life: 'The derogation of assertiveness as machismo,' wrote Didion, 'has achieved such currency that one imagines several million women too delicate to deal at any level with an overtly heterosexual man . . . Women who want not a revolution but romance, who believe not in the oppression of women but in their own chances of a new life in exactly the mould of their old life.' What many liberationalists were dreaming of was freedom in the guise of 'eternal love, romance, fun. The Big Apple.' And, as Didion proceeds to point out, 'these are relatively rare expectations in the arrangements of consenting adults, although not in those of children.'

Perhaps the unvarnished, grown-up gospel of feminism was just too difficult, perhaps, as Marghanita Laski wrote in the issue of *Country Life* that was published the day after the Wedding in July 1981, the Cinderella myth is the most necessary female myth.

Certainly to condemn such romance, even when it is clear that it is hardly realistic to sit around waiting for a handsome prince to turn up, appears to be pointing towards bleakness, loneliness, grim-faced isolation. The real world holds nothing that can match the dream – symbolized for Gatsby, the hero of the greatest romantic novel written this century, by the green light at the end of Daisy's dock:

Gatsby believed in the green light, the orgiastic future that year by year recedes before us. It eluded us then, but that's no matter – tomorrow we will run faster, stretch out our arms further . . . And one fine morning. So we beat on, boats against the current, borne back ceaselessly into the past.

Epilogue

An image is, at its simplest, a reflection, beaming back a copy of reality, bouncing it off a glass, filtering it through a lens or an eye. Or it is a projection on to a screen or imagination, a means of communication. It may, literally, be a re-presentation of the person or object reflected – in which case it may be elaborated upon, tricked out to make a point, to affirm identity, to illuminate or distort.

Gaze long or repeatedly into any of the available mirrors and you may begin to see something else: what you hope to see, what you fear, what you long for or loathe. Actual features become inseparable from the veil of ideas and emotions in which they are clothed, or through which they are viewed. The process of projection or reflection, identification and recognition goes on continually and intimately in all our lives, a necessary part of our nervous system, a vital element of communication, the very essence of perception. On a grand scale, images are created to express and promote cultural identity; to assert the spirit of the time. And that spirit is evoked more than anything else through the images – graven and otherwise – of its women. Ideas and visions of what a woman is, or should be, are so strong that they tend to swamp – with clothes and cosmetics and everything that goes to compose a stylistic or role identity – any sight of the woman as singular and individual. A woman is a cultural and social statement first, herself afterwards.

The faces of fashion and of instantly recognizable stereotypes – mothers, wives, careerists, grandmas and sex objects – gaze at us from advertisement hoardings and magazine pages; they smile and beguile us from television screens, and by announcing clearly *what* they are, they tell others what they may also be. In advertising, women's images are used to sell products; they are also used to sell identity – soap *and* reassurance.

This continues, even though the process is well understood, even though women themselves have tried with enormous energy to resist and change it, in spite even of the attempt in advertising itself to present a modern 'ambiguous' woman who cannot any more be simply defined in terms of her role. Strident complaints about stereotyping have been ineffective in everything except the creation of new images and stereotypes. The feminist bid for a kind of sexual or at least gender anonymity, the search for an image which was not concocted according to men's requirements, succeeded chiefly in creating a perception of feminism which is drab and dour at best, ugly and aggressive at worst. An image can be used to dismiss and de-value, just as it can to idealize or over-value.

This particular image has been seized on by the editorial side of the media. Journalists and scriptwriters bring to life an idea of feminism which may not be 'fair', and may not be 'true', but works potently in the public imagination. Likewise standards of beauty are more, not less uniform. Anna Ford, a British newscaster who in the Seventies became one of the most famous and fêted women in the country because she was beautiful and could read autocue smoothly, complained publicly and often about the way women, including herself, were judged by looks first, abilities afterwards. 'Body fascism', she called it crossly, but her imprecation had a hollow ring, and there were those who smiled knowingly at the sight of this butterfly wriggling on a pin. What did she want? Purdah? The pressures of being beautiful, of having a body or face which is also public property have never elicited much sympathy from men, nor indeed from women who tend rather to spend time and money trying to match up to the ideal.

Marina Warner, who has published, among other things, lengthy studies of the Virgin Mary and Joan of Arc, has written that 'the tradition of female allegory is underpinned by the assumption that woman is *tabula rasa*, on to which we inscribe meanings. She does not say her own name, or control her destiny; no person inhabits her body, only the ideal that someone has poured into it.' And of

such inpourings stars are born. A woman who rises as a star of her
time is one whose charisma and implicit emotional meaning is so
strong that she seems to sum up or enshrine our values, ideals and
deepest desires. She may do this by acting out fantasies on a stage or
in a film; she will do it most of all by simply *being*, and, above all,
her being is her looks.

The quintessential star of the post-Second World War period has
been, in one guise or another, the blonde. She has been the symbol
of fun and submissiveness, loving happy sexuality. To be blonde is
to be a man's woman, to be preferred and desired. Marilyn Monroe
was the luscious dream woman for a generation reconstructing its
home life after the trauma of war; the glorious piece of fluff. A little
later Brigitte Bardot was the plaything of new-found sexual emancipation, the sex kitten, best of baby dolls.

In reality, Monroe was dead at thirty-six, and while she lived
was haunted by a nightmare of finding herself twelve feet tall, and
stark naked in front of a gaping crowd. Bardot tried (with near
success) to commit suicide, and has latterly retreated into a secluded
retirement, seeming to prefer animals to people. These were women
trapped between the isolation of reality and their own images, far
more powerful than themselves.

Diana, Princess of Wales, combines the glamour of the movie star
with the power of the madonna: sexual yet untouchable. Her hair
becomes blonder, her dresses slinkier, her smile more dazzling; at
the same time, she is less vulnerable than any mere actress; she
recedes into and is sustained by a royal pageantry that was holding
and subduing audiences long before the cinema was invented. Tom
Nairn, the left-wing writer, complained in the pre-Diana days of
1977 that the British were the victims of a Disneyish charade and
that the monarchy's 'exaggerated popularity is the voice of still
active conservatism'. He also pointed out that the House of Han-
over, later Windsor, was chosen to be precisely that – a dynasty of
show-kings and queens that would swathe the structure of government in glamour but not interfere with its workings.

Diana is living up to the demands of this system better than
anyone the family has so far produced. She has shown an uncanny

ability to rise to the expectations of her public; 'spreading,' as one magazine had it, 'happiness wherever she goes.' She is the angel of redemption, the figurehead on the prow of the national ship, the Spirit of Ecstasy on the Rolls-Royce, the endlessly viewable heroine of an obsessively viewing age.

What the 'real' Diana sees in the eyes of those who press around her or in her own carefully and increasingly heavily made-up eyes, as flashed back at her from those magazine covers and newspapers, can only be guessed at, or speculated over, as if she really were the star of a television soap opera. What we project on to her, the demands made on her, are another matter. She has to be, first, a re-presentation to us, on a gold plate, of ideal love, beauty, youth and, now, sexuality. She must also appear as the quintessential happily married mother and wife.

She achieves all this, starring in what amounts to being a long-running silent movie, by appearing and gesturing and saying almost nothing. 'The eyes have it' someone wrote as a caption to an early shot of Diana peering out from under her fringe. They continue to speak volumes.

Marshall McLuhan famously declared in the Sixties that the medium was the message. In this case the Princess is the medium; messages are written all over her with fashion, make-up, dress codes and behavioural restrictions. We do not require footbinding or purdah, what we do require and what we ask is physical perfection and something that in a royal context is usually called 'radiance'. Thus she must not only shine, but glow.

Diana's clothes and discussion about them are the easiest form of access to her, a way of grabbing hold. Copying them or her hairstyle brings us closer. People who resemble her catch the eye: some of the television presenter Selina Scott's success came from her similarity; Catherine Oxenburg, who played Diana in a movie around the time of the wedding, arrived on the set of *Dynasty* with a royal advantage. Even George Michael, star of the pop group Wham!, knows

Diana's is essentially a middle-aged dream of glamour and safety; she may be teaching some 'born again good girls' to think middle-aged, too.

how to make the most of being a Di look-alike. In fact, Diana transcends her clothes – she dazzles in spite, rather than because of, them. 'To her fashion is just an accessory,' wrote an Italian commentator. 'Lamb dressed as mutton' snapped a British writer, critical of the over-age clothes she is forced into wearing in the cause of royal *dignitas*.

Diana's youth is undeniable, but admiring it can mean avoiding or dodging, or mentally cancelling out, less acceptable faces of youth. She can be our ambassadress visiting Italy or the United States; she cannot so easily perform the same function to the girl in the street. To her Diana can offer only dreams of true love and babies and pretty clothes; she cannot offer a credible vision of a future to those who suspect there will be none and who do not wish to wallow in the past.

The hard-edged, self-invented street-bred images that glare out of anti-establishment publications such as *The Face* have little truck with the Princess: the refusniks of our 'mainstream' culture fear the future and will not buy the present on anyone's terms but their own. They have, in their small corner, replaced the vapid face of fashion with a new scowly chic. If Jean Shrimpton could recall that in the Sixties she had only two expressions, 'vacant and very vacant', the fringe models of the Eighties might say that theirs are sulky and very sulky. Even back in the mainstream where the supergloss sisters of *Cosmopolitan* and its clones continue to smile gamely, the strain often shows. The bared white teeth and thickly coated lips set in a hungry smarl – somewhere between a smile and a snarl.

Diana is, to some extent, playing to a gallery of men and women older than herself. Hers is a middle-aged person's dream of glamour and safety, and by it she may be teaching some of the born-again good girls to think middle-aged too.

Colin McDowell reporting for the *Observer* on her fashion impact in Italy, regretted that she was 'a fashion-conscious princess who is not allowed to be fashionable'. She is also a young princess forbidden

The other Madonna: refusniks of mainstream culture choose their own stars and have replaced the vapid face of fashion with a new, scowly chic.

to be truly young. As McDowell noted, she patronizes dress-
makers, not designers: the stunning, adventurous, new British designers are out of bounds. No Body Map, no Hyper Hyper, no street
credibility. Katharine Hamnett, the British designer who sent message T-shirts round the world, says she knows Diana has some of her
clothes but that she never wears them in public.

The most devastating attack on Diana's dress code has come from
the highly influential *W*, the weekly offshoot from *Women's Wear
Daily*. When they published their gallery of 'Fashion Victims 1985'
the Princess was top of the list, meriting three pages of searing
full-colour exposure of her designer clothes at their worst. It was a
bitchy, but not untruthful, exercise and it was fascinating to see the
same old familiar pictures used to reinforce a critical commentary
rather than, as is usual in British magazines or books, in a sugary
celebration.

'Fashion Victim' was a taunt invented by *W*'s publisher John
Fairchild to designate women (and men) who try too hard, 'who
remind you of your grandmother's Christmas tree: too many lights,
too many bulbs and altogether too much tinsel. They suffer from
fashion blindness. FVs look in the mirror and see the fairest of them
all, when in fact the glass is about to crack.'

Most of the *W* designated species are rich in money and in years.
The 'Hall of Fame' includes Joan Collins and a whole gaggle of New
York socialites, all tricked out in buttons and bows, ruffles and rocks.
The verdict on Diana was simple: when she is dressed in simple,
casual clothes she looks terrific. 'On duty she exhibits all the symp-
toms of being a 23-year-old fashion victim, a sufferer from the all
too common disease of grabbing at every new look and trend
whether it suits her or not.' The worst outfit of the Italian tour, for
instance, was, according to *W*, a 'cardboard-stiff emerald green
checked coat with all the visual appeal of a horseblanket. This was
then given the coup de farce by the addition of a huge, amorphous,
emerald green hat.' There are, conceded *W*, some good designers in

Diana the Fashion Victim: wearing the coat that the American paper
W described as having the visual appeal of a horseblanket.

England who design for the Princess, but there are 'others who should stick to dressing the Queen Mother, not turning a young, ravishingly pretty princess into a middle-aged frump.'

All the same, on the same page, it is announced that Diana has a secret ingredient 'that no one can take away from her . . . a communicable charm which triumphs over the endless routine of her Royal public life.'

Why should she have been so tempted to clothe this charm according to such ageing lights?

Since the Second World War, in Western Society, female imagery has been filtered through the fashion industry, the cinema and advertising. Ideas of liberation may have sprung from changing social reality, from education and raised consciousness, but they were seized upon and tamed by commerce and marketing. 'Freedom' became a watchword – whether in relation to tampons or career opportunities – but paradoxically, passivity remained implicit, the anchor was never raised. Instead of a simple passivity, however, there arose the myth of the New Woman, or the Today Woman, one who had infinite capacity, could 'manage' home and career, who might truly 'have it all'.

Thus, while women were being described and describing themselves as 'liberated' and 'free', they were also still being presented as 'wanting' (both in the sense of 'lacking' and 'desiring') whether it was a man, home, orgasms, babies or just more lipstick. They became both consumer and consumed. Because, just at the moment when society seemed truly to be offering more choice and some genuine liberation, it was also, in its iconography, underscoring the old bind – with zombie-like models, plastic doll-women, ever smiling housewives. In the Eighties – and the age of the Princess – this renewed and glamorized passivity is more than anything else denying, or making impossible, true equality between the sexes.

It is not that men do not suffer from stereotyping – they do; but their role-images are usually to do with potency and sexual fantasy, or with simple heroic escapism (cowboy, warrior, sportsman, stud, etc.). When these dreams fail them and wimpishness or self-doubt threaten, they have the essential neutrality of maleness. At the end of the day, men are *it*, the norm, with, as British journalist Peter Martin has written, only God on their blind side, which goes some way to explain why Western men are often physically and socially confident to the point of blindness. Stand in any pub, restaurant or wine bar and see and hear them let go. It is nothing to do with economic or even emotional security: many of them may be broke or burdened with debts, bad marriages or sexual neuroses. What they have is a collective *image* security: they know what they are, without even thinking about it. Looks matter, but they do not expect to be judged by them. And they can still rely on women to adhere to *their* standards and expectations, in looks as in everything else.

And women work very hard to please, often on many fronts; in real life few women inhabit only one role or conform to one stereotype: the 'Modern Woman' if she can be defined at all is one who combines many roles and has many faces. In advertising nowadays they talk anxiously about the 'target' as being the 'ambiguous' or 'ambivalent' woman, one about whom you can't quite tell by looking at her whether she is more at home in the boardroom, kitchen or bedroom, or all three. This is hard to evoke visually and little tokens creep in: the dizzy blonde carrying an important briefcase, the svelte woman at a desk with shopping bag visible under it. It is even harder to live up to. Adam is still, given a few scars to his ego, still Adam. Eve has been shattered into a thousand pieces, some of them glittering. There seems to be an incurable need – maybe not just on the part of men – for this kind of fragmentation, for women to inhabit dreams and ideals, to guard the household gods.

A 'woman's right to choose' has become a matter of 'options'. Barbara Gordon at the end of her autobiography of breakdown, *I'm Dancing As Fast As I Can*, suddenly cannot blame herself, or her lover, or her doctors for her trials: 'I began to think a lot about how we keep changing our skins, shedding our fur like animals in the spring, spiraling, growing, assuming new roles. At first I thought it was because of our oestrogen cycle, but it is not menstrual, it's cultural. And our culture, like a giant supermarket, now offers a bewildering variety of choices for women.'

There have been, of course, no shortage of gurus and high

Flexible Fonda, inspiring a generation to aim for a body that can be slim and hard and fighting fit at fifty.